ALL FOR ART ❧
THE RICKETTS AND
SHANNON COLLECTION ❧

ALL FOR ART
THE RICKETTS AND
SHANNON COLLECTION
EXHIBITION SELECTED AND
CATALOGUE EDITED BY
JOSEPH DARRACOTT
FITZWILLIAM MUSEUM
CAMBRIDGE 9 OCTOBER–
3 DECEMBER 1979

CAMBRIDGE UNIVERSITY
PRESS CAMBRIDGE · LONDON ·
NEW YORK · MELBOURNE

FITZWILLIAM MUSEUM
CAMBRIDGE

Published by the Syndics of the Cambridge University Press
The Pitt Building, Trumpington Street, Cambridge CB2 1RP
Bentley House, 200 Euston Road, London NW1 2DB
32 East 57th Street, New York, NY 10022, USA
296 Beaconsfield Parade, Middle Park, Melbourne 3206, Australia

© Fitzwilliam Museum 1979

First published 1979

Printed in Great Britain at the
University Press, Cambridge

Library of Congress Cataloguing in Publication Data
Cambridge. University. Fitzwilliam Museum.
All for Art
1. Art – Exhibitions. 2. Ricketts, Charles S.,
1866–1931 – Art collections – Exhibitions. 3. Shannon,
Charles Hazelwood, 1863–1937 – Art collections – Exhibitions.
I. Darracott, Joseph. II. Title.
N5247.R5C35   1979   707'.4'02659   79-14089
ISBN 0 521 22841 7 hard covers
ISBN 0 521 29674 9 paperback

CONTENTS

PLATES 🙢

ABBREVIATIONS FOR CLASSICAL REFERENCES 🦎

Beazley, *A.B.V.*: J. D. Beazley, *Attic Black-Figure Vase-Painters* (Oxford 1956)

Beazley, *A.R.V.*: J. D. Beazley, *Attic Red-Figure Vase-Painters* (Oxford 1963)

Budde and Nicholls, *Sculpture*: Ludwig Budde and Richard Nicholls, *Catalogue of the Greek and Roman Sculpture in the Fitzwilliam Museum* (Cambridge 1964)

C.V.A. Cambridge II: Winifred Lamb, *Corpus Vasorum Antiquorum, Fitzwilliam Museum, Cambridge,* fascicule II: *The Ricketts and Shannon Collection* (Oxford 1936)

Greek Art, 1903: Burlington Fine Arts Club, *Exhibition of Ancient Greek Art, 1903* (London 1904)

Smith and Hutton, *Cook Collection*: C. H. Smith and C. A. Hutton, *Catalogue of the Antiquities (Greek, Etruscan and Roman) in the Collection of the late Wyndham Francis Cook, Esqre.* (London 1908)

FOREWORD

'Twin bedsteads of spotless white, two washstands, and, on the wall, drawings or prints of masters – such was the aspect which lent character to the cubicle shared by Shannon and Ricketts, those acolytes promoted by the highest of the lesser orders of art. Ricketts's lean face reminded one of Francis of Assisi or a van Eyck; Shannon was like one of Burne-Jones's Knights of the Round Table...Their flat was filled with exquisite things, Persian miniatures, Tanagra figures, Egyptian antiques, jewels and medals, which millionaires had overlooked. For genuine collectors are poor; they are seekers and men of knowledge guided by their taste.' (*Portraits of a Lifetime*, 1937)

Jacques-Emile Blanche has sketched for us the life-style of these devotees of art, devoted to each other; and he has painted the sum of their appearance on canvas (L8). Alphonse Legros by his appropriately exquisite pencil refined their refinement to one substance (L10,11). Edmund Dulac teased them in tempera as medieval saints (L12). We know them also as they saw themselves, fastidiously: Shannon the painter (L3), and Ricketts the illustrator (L7). This exhibition is designed to celebrate them and their taste. Unlike the brothers de Goncourt, they were working artists; and they were not rich.

Interest in their personalities, their collecting and the range of their achievement has revived during the past dozen years. In 1966 the Fitzwilliam put on a small centenary exhibition to commemorate Charles Ricketts, at whose death in 1931 the Museum had already received on loan an important part of what eventually enriched it six years after that on the death of Charles Shannon. For London last year an exhibition of lithographs by Shannon was offered at Taranman in the Brompton Road; and this year at the Orleans House Gallery in Twickenham the London Borough of Richmond upon Thames presented 'Charles Ricketts and Charles Shannon, an aesthetic partnership', to which we were pleased to lend some pieces of jewellery made by Ricketts.

Now there is to be a monograph. The author, Mr Joseph Darracott, is Keeper of the Department of Art at the Imperial War Museum. For many years he has researched his subjects, and the ambience in which they found their objects and their friends. We are delighted that he could accept in advance of the publication of his book our invitation to select and introduce an exhibition to be based on our holdings, not only of their own drawings, stage designs, prints, books, jewellery, and sculpture, but also of the old master drawings and antiquities which they prized. To these *desiderata* we have fortunately been able to add important loans, particularly a group of Japanese woodcuts from the British Museum; and the National Gallery, inhibited from lending the pride of the Ricketts and Shannon collection, the Piero di Cosimo *Lapiths and Centaurs*, since it is painted on a panel which has settled to full air-conditioning, kindly enables us to show a photograph enlarged to the original size of the painting. We are no less indebted to the other lenders to this exhibition, both private and public. From this Museum, we have supplied Mr Darracott with catalogue entries for the items which he has chosen; and the exhibition is indebted to the work of the Keeper Staff, past and present, in our Departments of Paintings and Drawings, of Applied Arts, of Antiquities, of Manuscripts and Printed Books, of Prints, and of Coins and Medals. From the Arts Council of Great Britain a substantial grant has defrayed considerably the costs of the exhibition. Again we are grateful to the Syndics and staff of the Cambridge University Press for undertaking publication of an exhibition catalogue for the Museum. Special thanks are due to Mr Duncan Robinson, who has co-ordinated the efforts required in combination to mount the exhibition, as well as to Mr Darracott himself.

MICHAEL JAFFÉ
Director

ACKNOWLEDGEMENTS

For loans: the Trustees of the National Portrait Gallery (L1, L2); the Trustees of the Tate Gallery (L4, L8, A1, A5); the Royal Academy of Arts (A2); the Atkinson Art Gallery, Southport (A6); the Trustees of the British Museum – Department of Prints and Drawings (A7, A15, A16), Department of Oriental Antiquities (212–23, 227–32); the Visitors of the Ashmolean Museum (A8); the Victoria and Albert Museum (A17); the Russell Cotes Art Gallery, Bournemouth (A21); the Scottish National Gallery of Modern Art (A22); private lenders (L6, A3, A4, A29).

For the use of copyright material: Miss Henriette Sturge Moore and Daniel Sturge Moore, Esq., Ricketts' literary executors; the National Gallery of Canada.

CHARLES RICKETTS AND
CHARLES SHANNON: CHRONOLOGY 🐍

1863 Charles Shannon born
1866 Charles Ricketts born
1880 Ricketts' mother died
1880s Ricketts and Shannon studied at the City and Guilds Technical
      Institute, Kennington Road, Lambeth. Shannon taught at
      Croydon School of Art; Ricketts did magazine illustrations
1887 Thomas Sturge Moore met Ricketts
1892 First issue of *The Dial*
1893 Ricketts' first books: Oscar Wilde's *Sphinx*, and *Daphnis and
      Chloe*
1894 Michael Field (Katherine Bradley and Edith Cooper) met
      Ricketts and Shannon, then living in The Vale, Chelsea. *Hero
      and Leander*
1896 Name adopted for the Vale Press
1898 Ricketts and Shannon moved to Richmond
1899 Michael Field in Richmond. Ricketts and Shannon visited Venice
1902 Ricketts and Shannon took a 21-year lease of a flat in Lansdowne
      House, built for artists by Edmund Davis
1903 Ricketts: *The Prado and its Masterpieces*
1904 *Vale Press Bibliography*
1906 Ricketts: exhibition of sculpture
1910 Ricketts: *Titian*
1911 Visit to Greece and Egypt
1913 Ricketts: *Pages on Art*. Death of Edith Cooper
1914 Ricketts and Shannon exhibited in New York. Death of
      Katherine Bradley
1915 Ricketts declined the Directorship of the National Gallery
1916 Shannon: Chantrey Bequest purchase
1917 Ricketts: *Don Juan* bought for Tate Gallery
1918 Sir Edmund Davis bought Chilham Castle; the keep given for
      life to Ricketts and Shannon
1923 Rickets and Shannon bought Townshend House, St John's
      Wood
1929 Shannon's accident
1931 Death of Ricketts
1937 Death of Shannon

LIVES 🙷

Charles Ricketts and Charles Shannon met in the 1880s, both of them being apprenticed as wood-engravers. At first Shannon taught at the Croydon School of Art, while Ricketts, who had a small allowance from his grandfather, earned some money from magazine and commercial illustration. It became their intention for Shannon, the more gifted painter, to establish his reputation while Ricketts made certain of their livelihood. This was the pattern of their lives in the 1890s, when various artistic ventures culminated in the establishment of the Vale Press.

Among the close friends of Ricketts and Shannon in the 1890s were the poets Katherine Bradley and her niece Edith Cooper, who together wrote under the name 'Michael Field', making a literary parallel to Ricketts' and Shannon's artistic partnership. For some years, after a period in Chelsea, the painters joined the poets to live near to each other in Richmond. The friendship endured to the deaths of Edith Cooper in 1913 and of Katherine Bradley in 1914, despite the poets' conversion to the Roman Catholic faith, which was especially far from Ricketts' pagan way of thought. Ricketts always admired Michael Field's poetry, and was glad to know that the two poets were recalled by his jewellery for them in the Fitzwilliam Museum.

A more famous friend of the early period was Oscar Wilde, who was kind to the young Ricketts, finding him work as a book designer, and who was a visitor to the artists' house in The Vale, Chelsea, which he described as 'the house in London where you will never be bored'. Other literary friends included Thomas Sturge Moore, Ricketts' literary executor and the author of the only monograph on Ricketts before this year. Sturge Moore as a writer on art reflects Ricketts' views, as did also Charles Holmes in his *Notes on the Science of Picturemaking* (1911). Holmes was the business manager for the Vale Press before taking up official positions, first at the National Portrait Gallery, and then as Director of the National Gallery.

The Vale Press suffered a fire in which many woodblocks were destroyed; the Press's bibliography was published in 1904. The artists turned to other activities. Shannon began to have a growing reputation as a portraitist, while Ricketts turned to painting and sculpture. His poetic and imaginative pictures did not come easily to him, and his sculpture, where he found himself more at home, was not a financial success. Instead he developed his gifts as a writer. Looking back at their

2

lives Ricketts saw the years before the war as outstandingly fruitful – from 1906 to 1908 'all sorts of interesting people turn up'.

Ricketts formed friendships with playwrights, actors and actresses in the pre-war years. George Bernard Shaw, Yeats, John Masefield, Lillah McCarthy and her husband Harley Granville Barker, and Mrs Patrick Campbell were among the people whom the artists knew well. As visitors to the theatre and to concerts the two artists enjoyed the best entertainment London had to offer, being especially enthusiastic about Diaghilev's Russian Ballet.

The war years were a period of depression and gloom. Like other artists they were involved in charity performances, giving pictures and other work to sales for the Red Cross or other funds. News of the war became a preoccupation, and events like Zeppelin raids over London held an unhappy fascination. It was in 1915 that Ricketts declined the Directorship of the National Gallery – a decision he afterwards regretted. His friend Cecil Lewis, a notable aviator and the author of *Sagittarius Rising*, wrote that Ricketts used to say that he had died during the war.

In the 1920s the two artists were both Royal Academicians, but Ricketts' main achievement was in the theatre. Since the years before the war some actresses had particularly wanted Ricketts to design for them, irrespective of who was responsible for the play as a whole. Ricketts had been involved in small-scale productions, but in the 1920s he took on major challenges – George Bernard Shaw's *Saint Joan*, a mystery play at Canterbury Cathedral for John Masefield, and the re-dressing of Gilbert and Sullivan's *Mikado*. He also published dialogues under the title *Beyond the Threshold*, a beautifully written book which suggests his responses to life. But part of the two artists' response to life was through art, and the collecting of art, which this exhibition can help to document.

Early in 1929, Shannon suffered a serious concussion when he fell whilst hanging a picture: he never recovered his senses. Ricketts did everything possible for his friend, making sure of his well-being by the sale of items from their collection. Ricketts died in 1931, Shannon in 1937.

L1 🐍 CHARLES SHANNON

The man in the Inverness cape
Oil on canvas. 953 × 990 mm
Collection: National Portrait Gallery

The portraits of Ricketts (L1) and Shannon (L2) were owned by Sir Edmund Davis.

3

L2 CHARLES SHANNON

The man in the black shirt, 1897
Oil on canvas. 928 × 962 mm
Collection: National Portrait Gallery

L3 CHARLES SHANNON

Self-portrait
Oil on canvas. 686 × 680 mm
Signed and dated 1917
Collection: Fitzwilliam Museum (no. 2294)
Literature: Fitzwilliam Museum, *Catalogue of Paintings* III (1977) pp.
218–19

L4 CHARLES SHANNON

Mrs Patrick Campbell, 1907
Oil on canvas. 1230 × 1090 mm
Collection: Tate Gallery (no. 2995)
Literature: Tate Gallery, *The Modern British Paintings, Drawings and
Sculpture* II (1964) pp. 614–15

L5 CHARLES SHANNON

Lucien Pissarro
Lithograph. 222 × × 186 mm
Collection: Fitzwilliam Museum (gift of Charles Shannon, 1917)

Lucien Pissarro (1863–1944), son of Camille Pissarro, was a close friend
of the artists in the nineties. The Brook type for Lucien Pissarro's Eragny
Press was based on Ricketts' Vale type. The decorative type and
ornaments used in this catalogue are set in the original Brook type.

L6 CHARLES SHANNON

The modeller
Lithograph. 182 × 187 mm
Collection: private

Shannon's first lithographic portrait was of Thomas Sturge Moore
(1870–1944), poet and wood-engraver.

L7 🦎 CHARLES RICKETTS

Self-portrait, *c.* 1899
Chiaroscuro woodcut. 337 × 255 mm
Collection: Fitzwilliam Museum (Charrington collection)

L8 🦎 JACQUES EMILE BLANCHE

Charles Ricketts and Charles Shannon, 1904
Oil on canvas. 920 × 730 mm
Collection: Tate Gallery (no. 4907)
Literature: Tate Gallery, *The Foreign Paintings, Drawings and Sculpture*
(1959) pp. 9–10

L9 🦎 WILLIAM ROTHENSTEIN 1872–1945

Ricketts and Shannon, 1897
Lithograph. 340 × 228 mm
Collection: Fitzwilliam Museum (given by the Friends of the Fitzwilliam
Museum, no. P.81-1943)

William Rothenstein gives a particularly interesting account of the
artists' early years in *Men and Memories*, vol. 1 (1931). He introduced
them to Katherine Bradley and Edith Cooper.

L10 🦎 ALPHONSE LEGROS 1837–1911

Charles Ricketts
Silverpoint on pink prepared paper. 276 × 219 mm
Signed, and dated 1896
Collection: Fitzwilliam Museum (no. 2095)
Exhibition: *Cent dessins français du Fitzwilliam Museum* (1976) repr. no.
57

This drawing and L11 record a friendship which helped to revive public
interest in Legros's work. As a teacher at the Slade School Legros was
a vital link between English and French art, but he was resolutely against
Impressionism.

L11 ✎ ALPHONSE LEGROS 1837–1911

Charles Shannon
Pencil. 314 × 229 mm
Signed, and dated 1897
Collection: Fitzwilliam Museum (no. 2096)
Exhibition: *Cent dessins français du Fitzwilliam Museum* (1976) repr. no. 56

L12 ✎ EDMUND DULAC 1882–1953

Ricketts and Shannon as medieval saints
Tempera on panel. 387 × 305 mm
Signed, and dated 1920
Collection: Fitzwilliam Museum (no. PD.51–1966)
Literature: Fitzwilliam Museum, *Catalogue of Paintings* III (1977) p. 68

L13 ✎ EDMUND DULAC 1882–1953

Antonio Cippico
Watercolour. 343 × 267 mm
Inscribed 'L'Italia sara sempre l'Italia / e gli Italiani saranno sempre Italiani'; signed, and dated '13
Collection: Fitzwilliam Museum (no. 2041)

The subject is the friend to whom Ricketts dedicated *Beyond the Threshold*.

L14 ✎ EDMUND DULAC 1882–1953

Grey phantasms of early morn
Pencil, pen and ink, crayon, and watercolour. 211 × 252 mm
Inscribed lower left 'To my friend / Charles Ricketts / Edmund Dulac / 17'
Collection: Fitzwilliam Museum (no. 2039)

The sitter on Ricketts is Sir Thomas Beecham and the figure at the end of the bed, Lady Cunard. The third figure may be Martin Birnbaum.

6

L15 🦎 REGINALD FAIRFAX WELLS 1877–1951

Charles Shannon
Bronze. H 406 mm
Collection: Fitzwilliam Museum (no. M.68–1937)

The sculptor's work impressed Ricketts at first sight in 1901, when he recorded seeing 'some remarkable work by a youngster, a pupil of Lanteri, who does terra-cottas, influenced by Meunier, but with a latent realistic sense which might stand him in good stead, or ruin him'.

L16 🦎 DISH

Tin-glazed earthenware, painted in shades of yellow, orange, green, blue, grey, and black. H 38 mm, D 425 mm
Inscribed 'Ecbbo factto li ffilole di / Niobbe 1584'
Collection: Fitzwilliam Museum (no. C.3.1937)

The subject is Apollo and the sons of Niobe. As can be seen from photographs of the houses in which the artists lived, they possessed decorative objects, silver, and furniture. These were mainly dispersed; only a few objects went to public collections.

L17 🦎 LOCKET

Gold or silver-gilt. H including ring for suspension 54 mm, D 38 mm
Interior of lid inscribed 'Hair of D. G. Rossetti / cut in 1877. / and of A. C. Swinburne / cut in 1870. / given to S. C. Cockerell / by W. M. Rossetti in 1910 / and by / Isabel Swinburne / in 1913.'
Collection: Fitzwilliam Museum (no. M/P.6.1937)

The locket was given by Sir Sydney Cockerell to Ricketts and Shannon in 1926, and Ricketts replied (18 December 1926), 'The touching little locket has arrived safely. I am greatly touched. With the advance of years these great men grow dearer to me as the present grows more trivial and unreal. I am convinced that Rossetti will seem a sort of Giorgione in the time to come and Swinburne the equal or brother of Shelley.'

ART

The careers of Ricketts and Shannon as artists began together in their student days, diverged as Shannon sought to establish himself as a painter, came together in the joint venture of the Vale Press, and then went in separate directions. When Charles Holmes met Ricketts and Shannon in 1892, they were 'settling down to an agreed programme which had in it something of the heroic'. Shannon had exhibited at the Grosvenor Gallery in 1887, but 'Shannon was not to exhibit again until he appeared as the complete and undeniable master, upon whose princely income Ricketts then proposed to live in ease for the rest of his life...[It was] upon Ricketts that the main burden was laid of providing for immediate wants, by drawing illustrations, advertisements or anything else which would bring in a little money.'

The Vale Press was a major venture of the years between 1896 and 1904, preceded by the notable editions of *Daphnis and Chloe* (1893) and *Hero and Leander* (1894). The woodblocks for the first took eleven months, the artists' aim being to achieve a degree of personal control in the Vale Press books to an extent that Ricketts felt had hitherto not been seen. This control was exercised over the design, lay-out, and production of the books, although the printing itself was done commercially, at the Ballantyne Press. Three types were used in Vale Press books: mainly the Vale type, occasionally the King's fount, and for Shakespeare the Avon fount, all designed by Ricketts. A fire at the Ballantyne Press destroyed woodblocks, limiting the possible extension of the Vale Press's activities. The type was thrown in the Thames, and the Press closed; the two artists turned to other activities.

In 1905 Shannon was sounded out by Sir George Clausen about standing for the Royal Academy, 'which plunged Shannon into astonishment and discomfort'. After 1910 the art world of London divided on the issue of modern art, crystallised by the Grafton Gallery exhibition of *Manet and the Post-Impressionists* organised by Roger Fry, and thereafter the traditional virtues of the art of Ricketts and Shannon became certain to be valued by established painters rather than the independents with whom they had been aligned in the 1890s against the Royal Academy. In the 1920s both artists were Royal Academicians, both represented in the Tate Gallery, Shannon by a Chantrey Bequest purchase, *The Lady with an Amethyst*, and Ricketts by *Don Juan*, which was bought and presented to the national collection by Sir Otto Beit.

8

Both artists were also represented in the Musée du Luxembourg, in a collection of British art presented by Sir Edmund Davis.

Ricketts made an assessment of their art in 1914, on the occasion of an exhibition of their work in New York. 'In some of the reviews we are both pitted against each other and classed in the wane of English Victorianism. The last accusation does not pain us. It is softened by strictures on Watts, Rossetti, Burne-Jones, with whom we are classed – as not reflecting the life of our time... The general strength of our work is in its design, in a regard for our material, and I believe in a certain decency of standard in aim.' This regard for material can be exemplified in the excellent use of lithography by Shannon, the careful study of oil-painting technique by both artists, and the feeling for bronze so evident in Ricketts' sculpture. The artists' aims can be understood partly through the collection of works of art from which this exhibition is selected, and partly suggested by half a sentence written by Ricketts: 'My personal belief is that great painting belongs to great artists, and that our best modern technicians are actually our imaginative painters, such as Watts, Puvis, Burne-Jones, Baudry and Gustave Moreau...' Add to this group of nineteenth-century artists a respect for the European tradition, particularly the art of the Italian Renaissance, and an enthusiasm for the qualities of design evident in Japanese prints: here are some points of reference for the allusive, sometimes learned, and always craftsmanlike work of the two artists.

In the 1890s the young Rothenstein had been impressed by the skill and patience of Ricketts and Shannon's wood-engraving: 'I had never come in touch with the Morris movement, and this craftsmanship side was new to me... From them I heard countless stories of Rossetti, of Burne-Jones, Holman Hunt, Millais and Madox Brown; in fact, at the time, I thought they would carry on the Pre-Raphaelite tradition.' In one sense they did, through their versatility, Ricketts turning with ease from engraving and illustration to jewellery, painting, writing on art, stage design. In the last activity there was a need for historical knowledge, dramatic sense, a fluency of visual ideas which Ricketts found (as Sturge Moore recorded) 'a holiday task'. His theatrical work earned him respect from writers, actors, and actresses, and his designs, acquired by the National Art-Collections Fund remain in galleries throughout the country as witness to his abilities. As for Shannon as an artist, there is in Ricketts' words 'Le charme d'une technique élégante et robuste, un sentiment du réel mais choisi, d'où la part du rêve n'est pas exclue... c'est un contemplatif qu'on dirait de passage, un rêveur doublé d'un travailleur qui ne s'émeut qu'aux exigences de son métier et devant l'idéal de son art.'

9

A1 🐟 CHARLES SHANNON

Lady with amethyst, 1915
Oil on canvas. 610 × 600 mm
Collection: Tate Gallery (no. 3152; Chantrey purchase, 1916)
Literature: Tate Gallery, *The Modern British Paintings, Drawings and Sculpture* II (1964) p. 615

A2 🐟 CHARLES SHANNON

Vanity and Sanity
Oil on canvas. 1050 × 1092 mm
Collection: Royal Academy (Diploma picture)

A3 🐟 CHARLES SHANNON

Romantic landscape, 1893
Lithograph. 225 × 217 mm
Collection: private

A4 🐟 CHARLES SHANNON

Lithograph in white line, 1891. 170 × 175 mm
Collection: private

A5 🐟 CHARLES RICKETTS

Don Juan
Oil on canvas. 1160 × 960 mm
Collection: Tate Gallery (no. 3221; presented in 1917)
Literature: Tate Gallery, *The Modern British Paintings, Drawings and Sculpture* II (1964) p. 558

A6 🐟 CHARLES RICKETTS

Bacchus in India
Oil on canvas. 1170 × 950 mm
Collection: Southport Art Gallery

A7 ⭐ CHARLES RICKETTS

Illumination for *Hero and Leander*, *c.* 1894
Gouache. 200 × 128 mm
Collection: British Museum

A8 ⭐ CHARLES RICKETTS

(a) Sphinx and Minotaur and (b) The Sphinx drinks, *c.* 1893
Pen and black ink on pink paper. (a) 193 × 169 mm; (b) 201 × 166 mm
Collection: Ashmolean Museum

A9 ⭐ CHARLES RICKETTS

The Sabbatai ring, *c.* 1904
Two-colour gold set with a gemstone. H 38 mm, W 25 mm
Collection: Fitzwilliam Museum (no. M.1–1914)

A10 ⭐ CHARLES RICKETTS

Blue bird brooch, 1899 (for Edith Cooper's birthday, 1900)
Gold, enamels, and gemstones. H 45 mm, W 28 mm
Collection: Fitzwilliam Museum (no. M.2–1914)

A11 ⭐ CHARLES RICKETTS

Pegasus pendant, 1901
Gold, enamels, gemstones, and pearls. H 102 mm, W 51 mm
Collection: Fitzwilliam Museum (no. M.3–1914)

This contains a miniature of Miss Edith Emily Cooper, who with her
aunt, Miss Bradley, wrote under the name of Michael Field.

A12 ⭐ CHARLES RICKETTS

Psyche pendant, 1903 (for the wedding of Mrs Sturge Moore)
Gold, enamels, and gemstones. H 128 mm, W 59 mm
Collection: Fitzwilliam Museum (no. M.4–1972)

A13 🦎 CHARLES RICKETTS

Pendant, 1903 (for the wedding of Mrs Sturge Moore)
Gold, enamels, pearls, and gemstones. H 83 mm
Collection: Fitzwilliam Museum (no. M.5–1972)

A14 🦎 CHARLES RICKETTS

Paolo and Francesca, 1909
Bronze. H 320 mm, L 530 mm
Collection: Fitzwilliam Museum (no. M.18–1972)

A15 🦎 CHARLES RICKETTS

Montezuma, *c.* 1925
Watercolour. 457 × 303 mm
Collection: British Museum

A16 🦎 CHARLES RICKETTS

Ecclesiastical vestments for Parsifal, *c.* 1921
Watercolour. 317 × 432 mm
Collection: British Museum

A17 🦎 CHARLES RICKETTS

Setting for *King Lear*, *c.* 1909
Watercolour. 367 × 521 mm
Collection: Victoria and Albert Museum

A18 🦎 CHARLES RICKETTS (see pl. 1)

Salome, 1919
Watercolour and body colour. 211 × 400 mm
Collection: Fitzwilliam Museum (no. 1646)

Stage setting for a production of Wilde's play planned for Tokyo.

A19 🦎 CHARLES RICKETTS

The Betrothal, *c.* 1920
Watercolour and body colour. 270 × 384 mm
Collection: Fitzwilliam Museum (no. 1647)

Stage setting for the production of Maeterlinck's play shown at the
Gaiety Theatre, London, in 1921.

A20 🦎 CHARLES RICKETTS (see pl. 2)

Saint Joan, *c.* 1923
Watercolour and body colour. 394 × 596 mm
Collection: Fitzwilliam Museum (no. 1649)

Curtain design for Shaw's play, produced in 1924 at the New Theatre.

A21 🦎 CHARLES RICKETTS

Costume design for the Doge in *The Merchant of Venice, c.* 1918
Watercolour. 394 × 305 mm
Collection: Russell Cotes Art Gallery, Bournemouth

A22 🦎 CHARLES RICKETTS

Costume design for *The Mikado, c.* 1926
Watercolour and indian ink over pencil. 508 × 365 mm
Collection: Scottish National Gallery of Modern Art (GMA 1013)

A23 🦎 LONGUS. *Daphnis and Chloe.* 1893

Printed on Van Gelder paper, Caslon type; woodcuts by Ricketts and
Shannon; bound in green buckram
Collection: Fitzwilliam Museum (bequeathed by J. R. Holliday, 1927)

A24   CHRISTOPHER MARLOWE and GEORGE CHAPMAN. *Hero and Leander.* 1894

The gold-tooled vellum binding designed by Charles Ricketts; monogrammed and dated 1894
Collection: Fitzwilliam Museum (bequeathed by J. R. Holliday, 1927)

A25   WILLIAM BLAKE. *The book of Thel: Songs of innocence and Songs of experience.* 1897

Printed on 'VP' watermarked paper, Vale type; frontispiece, borders, and initials by Ricketts
Collection: Sir William Russell Flint; Fitzwilliam Museum (purchased 1974)

A26   *The passionate pilgrim and The songs in Shakespeare's plays.* Edited by T. Sturge Moore. 1896

Printed on 'VP' watermarked paper, Vale type; woodcut and half border by Ricketts
Collection: Fitzwilliam Museum (bequeathed by J. R. Holliday, 1927)

A27   MICHAEL FIELD. *Fair Rosamund.* 1897 (see pl. 3)

Printed on 'VP' watermarked paper, Vale type; the border of roses by Ricketts
Collection: Fitzwilliam Museum (bequeathed by J. R. Holliday, 1927)

A28   DANTE GABRIEL ROSSETTI. *The blessed damozel.* 1898

Printed on vellum, Vale type; the binding, full red niger morocco, gold-tooled with a wheat-ear motif, designed by Ricketts and executed by J. Leighton; monogrammed
Collection: Fitzwilliam Museum (gift of Charles Ricketts, 1915)

A29   KING JAMES I OF SCOTLAND. *The Kingis Quair.* 1903

Printed on 'VP' watermarked paper, King's type; initial letter by Ricketts
Collection: private

14

Plate 1: Cat. no. A18

Plate 2: Cat. no. A20

ACT I

Scene I
Woodstock: masons rais~
ing the Labyrinth
Enter at a distance King Henry,
Sir Topaz, and Mavis

Ist MASON

YONDER
IS
THE
KING.

IInd MASON
He's aged of late.
Ist MASON
Ay, ay! about the face;
his fiery hair
Is dimmed as if by smoke;
his eyes are hollow,
Yet is he stout in body;
well~nigh young.

Plate 3: Cat. no. A27

COLLECTING 🐍

Ricketts and Shannon started collecting as students, and continued all their lives. Thomas Sturge Moore well depicts their early days: he wrote, 'The first floor front in the Kennington Road, where in tête-à-tête I first trembled lest the minutes were going too fast, had walls over which brown paper had been tacked to hide a hideous pattern; on this were pinned photographs by artists like those named above (Paul Baudry, Puvis de Chavannes, Gustave Moreau, Rossetti, Watts, Carpeaux, Rodin), sources of inspiration which then had no commercial value; but in bulky albums and worn portfolios were collections of the work of illustrators, rummaged from bookstalls, the Pre-Raphaelites, Boyd Houghton, Keene, alongside of Willette and Menzel or Blum, Brennan, Howard, Pile and Abbey.' Original works by the artists who inspired them in student days as well as by those who were useful to them are to be found in the collection.

At Shannon's death in 1937 the collection contained more than a thousand items, the majority of which were bequeathed to the Fitzwilliam, although more than three hundred Japanese prints went to the British Museum. The bequest reflected personal friendships, with Laurence Binyon at the British Museum and with Sydney Cockerell at the Fitzwilliam. In 1918 Shannon visited Cambridge, was much impressed with the Fitzwilliam, and felt that the collection should be kept together there. Both artists made identical wills soon afterwards. Some losses from the collection were sustained to pay Shannon's medical expenses – some notable Persian drawings were sold, for example – but nevertheless the collection is an outstanding one. Its scope is remarkably wide and it includes some of the best examples of the draughtsmanship of artists as important as Titian, Rembrandt, Rubens, and Watteau, in addition to those 19th-century artists who are mentioned by Sturge Moore. The range of their collecting also included Egyptian and classical antiquities, which they were buying from the 1890s: in 1897, for example, Ricketts wrote, 'There is a sale of classical antiquities coming on that will necessitate our presence as we want if possible to possess other cups that belonged to beautiful women, victorious prizemen, dancers, etc.' In the following year he wrote to refuse an evening invitation, 'We dread the late trains for the Iconoclast walks at dusk and we keep secret Tanagras hidden in cupboards.' When they were able to afford to do so, the artists went to Greece and Egypt, where they bought some of their antiquities: the majority, however, came either from the sale rooms or from London dealers. Cockerell was one of their friends who could appreciate their purchases, and several letters of collecting gossip remain. In 1912 Cockerell had arranged to visit Lansdowne House. Ricketts wrote with a lightness of touch to apologise for not being at home: 'The maid has instructions to give you tea. You will find the new Egyptian things and the new Intaglios in the drawers of the new case. The fine Greek vase is in the lower shelf of the old case (window corner). The new Mycenaean vase (with a piece of foot broken off by Clytemnestra's parlour-maid) is also in the old case, unless it is basking on one of the tables.' Two years later Ricketts wrote about the art dealer W. T. Ready, 'I was genuinely cut up at his death, though it saves me from the only man whose insight I feared. The last time I saw him he said, "After all, no one in London has your knowledge." This compliment charmed me, coming from a very British Britisher and from a man whose exact and technical knowledge far exceeded mine.'

Collecting antiquities at the turn of the century was not impossibly expensive, and the same was true of Japanese prints. To distinguish between the separate tastes of Ricketts and Shannon is seldom possible, but Shannon was especially active in buying Japanese art. In 1914 Ricketts wrote in a letter to Cockerell, 'Shannon has greatly added to our Japanese print department: our Harunobus are now more numerous and of a higher quality than those belonging to Harmsworth or the British Museum Print Room.' The two artists rightly prided themselves on their prints by this early master, and also on their holdings of Utamaro and Hokusai. Preference for these artists echoes the enthusiasm of the de Goncourt brothers, with whose way of life a comparison is certainly apt. Edmond de Goncourt wrote books on both Utamaro and Hokusai, in which there are admirable descriptions of the subjects of the prints; but for Ricketts and Shannon the attraction of Japanese art was not just its strangeness, but the qualities of the design: as Ricketts wrote in 1900, 'I think, at their best, that nothing quite touches a first-rate Jap print, excepting a good Greek Kylix or first-rate Tanagra: even the latter hardly compare; only the masterpieces of the greatest masters go beyond: picked Titians or Rembrandts, or world-famous frescoes.' The comparisons are interesting; they reveal a breadth of interest similar to the taste which furnished the de Goncourt home.

One of the intriguing questions about the artists' taste concerns the distinction they make between what was art and what was not. Antiquities might be on the borderline. In 1905 Ricketts was writing, 'I forget if we had got two charming pots of Rhodian ware when you were still with us, they are only nice, not art, but quite charming.' There is also the question about what was worth collecting; here Ricketts was more tempted to buy objects, say Persian ceramics, while Shannon hoped for drawings, the main strength of their collection. Paintings

18

were also always too expensive, and meant sacrifices. The Pièro di Cosimo painting in the National Gallery, *Lapiths and Centaurs*, is a case in point, since it was clearly a major picture which could have found a place in the Louvre, where it was refused just before the artists purchased it in 1904 for £700. In 1915, in a period of depression, Ricketts thought of selling the picture and going to Italy; but it was kept, and bequeathed to the National Gallery. Other paintings of importance were not kept when financial difficulties arose – a painting by Puvis de Chavannes was sold when the artists bought their house in St John's Wood; a painting by Daumier, bought in 1905, was no longer in their collection at the time of Shannon's death. Paintings kept, by Delacroix or Alfred Stevens, for example, therefore have special significance.

At more than 360, the English drawings outweigh the foreign schools in number. There are three particularly large groups: by Burne-Jones, by Ernest Cole, and by Alfred Stevens. This reflects both personal interest and the chance of the art market. Drawings by Burne-Jones were bought from his studio collection after his death; Cole was a protégé; and the drawings by Stevens came up in the sale room. The examples selected for this exhibition are chosen to illustrate each artist's range; they are matched in quality by many not included. The Pre-Raphaelites are particularly well represented. Rossetti, a hero of Ricketts, features both the charming personal studies of Elizabeth Siddal and also the magnificent *Mary Magdalene at the door of Simon the Pharisee*, a drawing which was considered lost until Charles Ricketts rediscovered it and purchased it, at some time before 1890. Eighteenth-century England also appears in eighteen drawings by Thomas Rowlandson. It may seem surprising that there are relatively few drawings by the artists' contemporaries – such purchases as were made were often to encourage students like Cole or the young Augustus John.

The French drawings owned by Ricketts and Shannon included fine examples by Watteau, but the 19th-century drawings demonstrate their taste, and are echoed in their own artistic practice. The list is almost a roll-call of French art of the century. Delacroix, Barye, Millet, Puvis de Chavannes, Rodin – but it stops short of the Impressionists, for whose work Ricketts had no sympathy. Landscape art was for him, as for Delacroix, 'the minor art of a specialist', an opinion explaining the very small number of landscapes in the collection.

That Ricketts was not unable to respond to landscape can be seen by the inclusion of Rubens' *Path Bordered by Trees*, but figure subjects were more decidedly within the artists' canon. It is in this field that the two collectors scored some of their most remarkable successes, acquiring drawings by Titian, Tintoretto, or Rembrandt. Ricketts had an excellent eye. Not all the attributions of drawings to particular old masters are upheld by modern scholarship, but it is often the case that an instinct for quality anticipated a documented conclusion. Ricketts was of the same generation as Bernard Berenson, for whom he had some respect; but for mechanical or over-dogmatic pseudo-scholarship he had scorn: in the introduction to his book on Titian he wrote, 'the dates given to pictures must in most cases be accepted as a symbol of their relation to each other, as I would be the last to imagine that the exact year or month has been revealed to me by some divine revelation'. In private he was even more outspoken: 'I have noticed that the man who takes up art criticism in the newest phase of "attribution" or rather "disattribution" is usually endowed with that visual sensibility which makes him helpless to distinguish between a muffin and a crumpet when he sees them side by side.'

The catalogue entries of the drawings here are based upon the admirable internal work of the Fitzwilliam Museum. They attempt to summarise present knowledge, without giving a full discussion of differing views, for which the specialist reader is referred to recent catalogues. Was Shannon right and Ricketts wrong about their drawing now ascribed to Verrocchio, but believed by Shannon to be by Leonardo? Is the Dürer landscape entirely by him, and does Rembrandt's *Supper at Emmaus* betray any sign of another hand? What of the drawings by Jordaens, van Dyck, and Rubens? Are we looking at the missing van Dyck of *Archbishop Laud*, or a studio repetition? Whatever the answers, there is no doubt that all of these form part of a remarkable collection, which constitutes one of the major benefactions to the Fitzwilliam Museum. This legacy is for all to see, and of the two men who gave it, the words of Eric Brown, Director of the National Gallery of Canada where Ricketts was adviser, are appropriate. He wrote at Ricketts' death: 'No one living had a greater sensitiveness towards the forms of art he particularly appreciated, and few ever possessed greater knowledge of subjects he chose to make his own, such as 15th and 16th century Italian pictures, old master drawings, costume of all ages, Japanese prints and drawings, and everything to do with the arts of wood engraving, fine printing and stage design.'

All works in these sections belong to the Fitzwilliam Museum, with the exception of the oriental works in the British Museum.

EGYPTIAN ART

1 TWO JARS

Dolomite(?). H 95 mm, D 141 mm and H 53 mm, D 93 mm
Dynasties II–III, 29th–27th centuries BC
Collection: Ricketts and Shannon (nos. E.35h.1937 and E.35c.1937)

The jars were used for cosmetics.

2 TWO VASES

Anhydrite. H 94 mm and H 42 mm
Dynasty XII, 1991–1785 BC
Collection: Ricketts and Shannon (nos. E.54.1937 and E.51.1937)
Exhibition: London, Goldsmiths' Hall *Treasures of Cambridge* (1959) no. 431
Literature: C. Winter, *The Fitzwilliam Museum* (1958) p. 28 with pl.; compare Fr. W. von Bissing, *Catalogue général des antiquités du Musée du Caire: Steingefässe* (Vienna 1907) p. 102, no. 18506, pl. VIII

The larger vase is from Akhmîm in Upper Egypt. It has, unusually, a pouring lip, and a body enclosed by two vultures, carved in relief with eyes of mother-of-pearl. Vultures were a symbol of the kingship of Egypt, and here they hold in their claws a hieroglyphic sign representing the world encircled by the sun, and ruled by the king. In Carl Winter's book the vase is dated to the Protodynastic period; however, the material and shape suggest a later time. The squat vase was used for the eye cosmetic, kohl, and has a separate rim.

3 TOILET STICK

Ivory. L 137 mm
Dynasties XVIII–XIX, *c.* 1550–1196 BC
Collection: Ricketts and Shannon (no. E.97.1937); bought at Sotheby's, Cat. 12–14 and 17–21 July 1911, no. 879, pl. XXI; formerly Hilton Price collection
Exhibition: London, Burlington Fine Arts Club *Ancient Egyptian Art* (1922) p. 62 (24)
Literature: compare J. D. Cooney in *Ancient Art: The Norman Schimmel Collection*, ed. Oscar White Muscarella (Mainz 1974) no. 175; I. Wallert, *Der verzierte Löffel, seine Formgeschichte und Verwendung in alten Ägypten* (Wiesbaden 1967), p. 86, p. 7(C6)

Possibly the handle of a cosmetic spoon. The head, carved in the form of an ibex, is joined to the shaft with a wooden peg. The pink paint may be of recent origin.

4 COSMETIC BOX

Wood. L 165 mm
Dynasties XVIII–XIX, *c.* 1550–1196 BC

Collection: Ricketts and Shannon (no. E.47.1937); bought at Sotheby's, Cat. 12–14 November 1917, no. 49; formerly Grenfell collection

The box, in the form of a duck, is from Thebes. The duck's wings, swivelling on pins, form the lid. The box was made in two parts joined at the base of the neck, and the lower beak is missing. The protruding tongue is painted red, and the eyes, feathers of head and body are represented in inlays of Egyptian blue (see cat. no. 17)

5   JEWELLERY

Gold inlaid with jasper, felspar, glazed frit, Egyptian blue, and glass.
(a) L 32 mm; (b) L 20 mm
(a) Dynasty XVIII, *c.* 1550–1305 BC; (b) Original date probably Middle Kingdom, 20th–19th centuries BC
Collection: Ricketts and Shannon (nos. E.86a.1937 and E.86b.1937)

(a) is a segment from a bead collar in the form of a lotus petal. (b) has the sun, uraeus snakes, and life symbols arranged as a pendant. The centre-piece with glass inlay was a later addition.

6   INLAY IN THE FORM OF THE GOD BES

(a) Ebony. (b) Ivory. H 108 mm
Dynasties XVIII–XIX, 1550–1196 BC
Collection: Ricketts and Shannon (nos. E.67c.1937 and E.68.1937)

Inlays from furniture or boxes. Bes, a beneficent demon associated with music, dancing, children, and women, has a composite identity represented by a dwarf's body, lion's mane and tail, and lotus head-dress.

7   FURNITURE INLAY

Inlaid bronze. H 230 mm
Dynasties XXII–XXIII, *c.* 9th–8th centuries BC
Collection: Ricketts and Shannon (no. E.17.1937); bought at Sotheby's, Cat. 26 June–6 July 1922, no. 1226, pl. XXXVI; formerly Macgregor collection

An offering-bearer carries an ibex over his shoulder, while another walks beside him. The man's dress, wig, and pose show a mixture of Egyptian and Phoenician iconography.

8   LION

Rudite limestone. L 64 mm
Dynasties I–II, *c.* 2955–2635 BC
Collection: Ricketts and Shannon (no. E.36.1937); bought at Sotheby's, Cat. 12–14 and 17–21 July 1911, no. 119; formerly Hilton Price collection
Exhibition: London, Burlington Fine Arts Club *Ancient Egyptian Art* (1922) p. 5 (22)

This gaming piece is from Nagada. The forepaws of the recumbent lion have broken off. The simple but strong modelling and the asymmetry of the face are characteristic of sculptures of this early period.

Ricketts wrote to Sir Sydney Cockerell that he had spent too much at this Egyptian sale. On 13 July he wrote, 'I am just back from a tiring day at Sotheby's, where everything I wanted was bought by Kalebdjian for Paris, at prices so indecent that my christian pen refuses to write them. I have however secured some nice odds and ends; two of them are more – in fact, of their kind, museum pieces. One of them is a small lion in spotty stone, "early-dynasty" period, the only others I have noticed are in Cairo...'

9   HEAD OF A WOMAN

Painted pink limestone. H 72 mm
End of Dynasty IV, *c.* 2490 BC
Collection: Ricketts and Shannon (no. E.27.1937)
Exhibition: London, Burlington Fine Arts Club *Ancient Egyptian Art* (1922) p. 96 (15)
Literature: compare W. Stevenson Smith, *A History of Egyptian Sculpture and Painting in the Old Kingdom* (1946) p. 42, pl. 16 (c)

The close-cropped hair is painted black, and the skin yellow, in keeping with Egyptian conventions. The paint has been applied over a thin layer of plaster.

10   HEAD AND SHOULDERS OF A MAN

Painted wood. H 128 mm
End of Dynasty VI, *c.* 2140 BC
Collection: Ricketts and Shannon (no. E.41.1937)

The wooden pins which joined the arms to the body are still in place

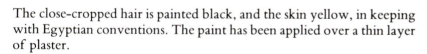

in the shoulders. The wig, brows, outlines of the eyes, and pupils are painted black. The face and body were originally covered with a thin white wash, and on the finely modelled back there are traces of red, which was the original body colour.

11 ✒ STATUE OF AN OFFICIAL (see pl. 4)

Plastered and painted wood. H 550 mm
Dynasty VI or a little later, *c.* 23rd century BC
Collection: Ricketts and Shannon (no. E.40.1937)

The staff in the man's left hand is restored. The small wooden peg projecting from the right side of the head and the adjacent area of discoloration suggest that there was originally a sidelock, the insignia of certain priesthoods. A short pleated kilt with projecting triangular fold and a bead collar knotted with string were worn. The layer of plaster is exceptionally thick, perhaps to cover defects in the wood, and it has obliterated the finer modelling of the torso. However, the face, with its plump cheeks, slightly bulbous eyes and full, curved mouth, is that of an individual, albeit an anonymous one.

12 ✒ STATUETTE OF A STANDING MAN

Ebony. H 128 mm
Late Dynasty VI – Dynasty XI, *c.* 2140–1991 BC
Collection: Ricketts and Shannon (no. E.39.1937)
Literature: compare G. Steindorff, *Catalogue of the Egyptian Sculpture in the Walters Art Gallery* (Baltimore 1946) pp. 34–5, no. 76, pl. XIV

The arms were carved separately, and a hole in the clenched right hand originally held a staff. There are projections on the bottom of the feet for insertion into a base.

13 ✒ STATUETTE OF A STANDING MAN

Limestone. H 88 mm
Late Dynasty XII – Dynasty XIII, 1842–*c.* 1650 BC
Collection: Ricketts and Shannon (no. E.25.1937)

Broken off just below the waist. The man wears a shoulder-length wig and a long kilt knotted just above the waist. The figure is supported by a rectangular back pillar running from the bottom edge of the wig.

24

14 UPPER PART OF AN USHABTI OF AN UNKNOWN MAN

Black steatite. H 72 mm
Dynasty XIX, Sethos I – Ramesses II, 1305–1224 BC
Collection: Ricketts and Shannon (no. E.56.1937)

The figure wears an elaborately pleated sleeved tunic, a bead collar, and a pendant, yet carries two hoes and, on his left shoulder, a seed bag for agricultural duties to be carried out in the next world (see cat. no. 15). The quality of this sculpture is outstanding: the contours of the body under the thin cloth are expressed as clearly as details of face and wig.

15 USHABTI OF DHUTMOSI

Limestone. H 176 mm
Dynasty XIX, 1305–1196 BC
Collection: Ricketts and Shannon (no. E.34.1937)

Dhutmosi was a priest in the temple of Thoth. Ushabtis were magical figures placed in tombs, which were intended to take the deceased person's place in the performance of unpleasant duties in the next world.

16 YOUNG BOY OR HARPOCRATES

Limestone. H 106 mm
Middle Ptolemaic period, *c.* 3rd century BC
Collection: Ricketts and Shannon (no. E.32.1937)

This conventional figure of a plump young boy wearing the sidelock of youth may represent the god Horus as a child, who was called Harpocrates by the Greeks. The statuette is supported by a back pillar with a trapezoid top.

17 VOTIVE STATUETTE OF A NAKED GIRL

Egyptian blue. H 106 mm
Ptolemaic period, 332–30 BC
Collection: Ricketts and Shannon (no. E.83.1937); bought at Sotheby's, Cat. 16–19 July 1912, no. 223, pl. v; formerly Kennard collection
Literature: compare B. von Bothmer, *Egyptian Sculpture of the Late Period*, Brooklyn Museum (1960) no. 95, pp. 119–21, pls. 88–9; G.

Roeder in *Studies Presented to F. Ll. Griffiths* (1932) pp. 332–40, pls. 52–3. For Egyptian blue, see A. Lucas, *Ancient Egyptian Materials and Industries*, ed. J. Harris (1962) pp. 340–4; F. R. Matson in E. Schmidt, *Persepolis 2* (Chicago 1957) pp. 133ff; R. H. Brill in A. L. Oppenheim *et al.*, *Glass and Glassmaking in Ancient Mesopotamia* (Corning, N.Y. 1970)

The statuette is moulded and finished by hand. The delicate modelling of the body and the strong personality visible in the face are worthy of a life-size sculpture. The rectangular back pillar, which starts just below the back of the hair, is pierced for suspension.

18   WINGED ISIS

Bronze. H 180 mm
Dynasties XXV–XXVI, *c.* 745–525 BC
Collection: Ricketts and Shannon (no. E.4.1937)

This was probably originally part of a group. The usual disc and horns worn by the goddess and seen in cat. no. 19 are missing. The figure can be compared with the goddesses found guarding the canopic shrine of Tutankhamun.

19   ISIS AND HORUS

Cast bronze. H 226 mm
Dynasties XXV–XXVI, *c.* 745–525 BC
Collection: Ricketts and Shannon (no. E.3.1937); bought at Sotheby's, Cat. 26 June – 6 July 1922, no. 1240; formerly Macgregor collection

An exceptionally fine example of a common subject, Isis suckling the infant Horus, who bears the insignia of kingship on his brow in addition to the child's sidelock. The pose is a source of the Virgin and Child in Christian iconography.

20   WOMAN CARRYING BES

Bronze. H 101 mm
Dynasties XXV–XXVI, *c.* 745–525 BC
Collection: Ricketts and Shannon (no. E.6.1937); bought at Sotheby's, Cat. 26 June – 6 July 1922, no. 1310, pl. XXXV; formerly Macgregor collection
Literature: G. Roeder, *Ägyptische Bronzefiguren* VI, *Mitteilungen aus der*

26

Ägyptischen Sammlung (Berlin 1956) p. 447; W. R. Dawson in *Journal of Egyptian Archaeology* XVI (1930) p. 143; K. Parlasca in *Mitteilungen des Deutschen Archäologischen Institutes, Athenische Abteilung* 68 (1953) pp. 132–3

The god's head-dress is now missing. Bes (see cat. no. 6) was venerated as the protector of women, especially during childbirth. The statuette may have been a thank-offering.

21   GRASSHOPPER

Solid-cast bronze. L 99 mm
Dynasty XXVI, 664–525 BC
Collection: Ricketts and Shannon (no. E.9.1937)
Literature: *Shell Magazine* XLIII (1963) p. 232 and pl. 232

The 'Field of Grasshoppers' was one of the more pleasant regions of the next world. The naturalistic detail of wings and feet, added after casting, is particularly fine.

22   CENSER INSCRIBED WITH THE NAME
     OF KING AMASIS

Hollow-cast bronze. L 398 mm
Reign of King Amasis, 570–526 BC
Collection: Ricketts and Shannon (no. E.13.1937); probably bought between 1922 and 1924 from the Rev. and Mrs Randolph Berens
Exhibition: London, Burlington Fine Arts Club *Ancient Egyptian Art* (1922) p. 108 as Berens collection
Literature: compare G. Roeder, *Ägyptische Bronzefiguren* VI, *Mitteilungen aus der Ägyptischen Sammlung* (Berlin 1956) pp. 432–3; A. St G. Caulfield, *The Temple of the Kings at Abydos*, Egyptian Research Account (London 1902) pl. XVI,7

The censer was made in three parts. The cartouche-shaped box in which the incense pellets were stored and the figure of the kneeling king were soldered into place, and the outstretched hand on which the pellets were

27

burnt (now missing) was riveted on to the holder. The inscription giving the name and epithets of the king is incised. The royal figure, not necessarily Amasis himself, is present because the box is the same shape as the framework, called a cartouche, within which royal names are invariably written. Several examples of this type of censer exist, but because of its quality and the inscription this is an exceptional example.

23 ✍ FORKED BUTT OF A CEREMONIAL STAFF

Bronze, with a modern repair in plaster. H 270 mm
New Kingdom or later, mid 16th to mid 8th century BC
Collection: Ricketts and Shannon (no. E.14.1937); bought at Sotheby's, Cat. 26 June – 6 July 1922, no. 1184, pl. XXXI; formerly Macgregor collection

The cow's head shown in relief suggests the staff was used in the celebration of the cult of the cow goddess, Hathor. The decoration represents leather thonging.

CLASSICAL ART

24 ✍ LONG-HAIRED YOUTHS AND SMALL PANTHERS (see pl. 5)

Cast bronze. H 155 mm forming the handles of a bronze amphora
Etruscan (Vulci ?), earlier 5th century BC
Collection: Ricketts and Shannon (nos. GR.105–6.1937); bought at Christie's, Cat. 14–16 July 1923, p. 26, no. 123 with pl. facing; formerly Cook collection
Exhibition: *Greek Art, 1903*, p. 60, nos. 92–3, pl. LXV
Literature: Smith and Hutton, *Cook Collection*, p. 119, no. 63, pls. XL and XLI

25 ✍ HERAKLES

Cast bronze statuette, possibly from a candelabrum. H 106 mm
Etruscan, *c.* late 4th – early 3rd centuries BC
Collection: Ricketts and Shannon (no. GR.104.1937)

26 🐚 ATHENA

Cast bronze votive statuette. Feet, spear, shield, and top of plume missing. P H 102 mm
Probably Attic, *c.* 500 BC
Collection: Ricketts and Shannon (no. GR.108.1937)

27 🐚 PERSEPHONE

Cast bronze votive (?) statuette, mounted on a non-pertinent ancient base. H (base excluded) 121 mm
North-east Peloponnesian, *c.* 470–460 BC
Collection: Ricketts and Shannon (no. GR.107.1937); formerly Tyszkiewicz collection
Exhibition: *Greek Art, 1903*, p. 41, no. 20, pl. XLVIII
Literature: *Apollo* LXXXIII (1966) p. 115, fig. 7

28 🐚 RECLINING SATYR

Cast bronze statuette, probably from the shoulder of a krater. L 56 mm
Corinthian (?), *c.* mid 6th century BC
Collection: Ricketts and Shannon (no. GR.109.1937)

29 🐚 HEAD OF AN AMAZON (?), FROM A BATTLE SCENE

Pentelic marble fragment, possibly from a high relief. P H 156 mm
Attic, 3rd–2nd centuries BC (?)
Collection: Ricketts and Shannon (no. GR.97.1937)
Literature: Budde and Nicholls, *Sculpture*, p. 41, no. 70, pl. XXIII

30 🐚 SMALL PORTRAIT OF THE EMPEROR CALIGULA (AD 37–41)

Cast bronze, probably from a small bust. H 42 mm
Collection: Ricketts and Shannon (no. GR.111.1937)
Literature: B. Schneider, *Studien zu den kleinformatigen Kaiserportraits von den Anfängen der Kaiserzeit bis ins dritte Jahrhundert* (Munich 1976) pp. 44–5 with pl. facing

31 🐟 TIBERIUS, EMPEROR AD 14–37

Glazed faience. H 72 mm
Collection: Ricketts and Shannon (no. GR.115.1937); bought at Christie's, Cat. 14–16 July 1925, p. 35, no. 179 with pl. facing; formerly Robinson and Cook collections
Literature: Smith and Hutton, *Cook Collection*, p. 65, no. 279, pl. XII; B. Schneider, *op. cit.* p. 33

This outstandingly fine Romano-Egyptian profile portrait dates from the beginning of Tiberius' reign.

32 🐟 MESSALINA (?), EMPRESS AD 41–8

Green jasper. P H 52 mm
Collection: Ricketts and Shannon (no. GR.116.1937); formerly Robinson and Cook collections
Literature: Smith and Hutton, *Cook Collection*, p. 64, no. 272, pl. XII

This is metropolitan Roman work. The type corresponds with the Paris cameo of Messalina, but has also been claimed as the elder Agrippina.

33 🐟 DEIFIED CHILD PORTRAIT

Chalcedony. H 60 mm
Roman, 2nd century AD
Collection: Ricketts and Shannon (no. GR.114.1937); formerly Bourguignon and Cook collections
Literature: Smith and Hutton, *Cook Collection*, p. 64, no. 275, pl. XIII

The child is depicted as a Season or Cupid, and the wings were subsequently cut away.

34 🐟 HERAKLES AND CENTAUR

Fragment of shallow agate bowl carved with relief figures. P H 35 mm
Roman, *c.* early 1st century AD
Collection: Ricketts and Shannon (no. GR.112.1937)

35 🐦 SEATED GODDESS

Terracotta statuette. H 122 mm
Attic, c. 500 BC
Collection: Ricketts and Shannon (no. GR.87.1937)

36 🐦 MIDDLE-COMEDY ACTOR

In the role of a fat parasite
Terracotta statuette. H 110 mm
Attic (or Corinthian derived from Attic), mid 4th century BC
Collection: Ricketts and Shannon (no. GR.85a.1937)
Literature: J. Chesterman, *Classical Terracotta Figures* (London 1974) p.
43, fig. 40; T. B. L. Webster, rev. J. R. Green, *Monuments Illustrating
Old and Middle Comedy* (London 1978) p. 55

37 🐦 NEW-COMEDY ACTOR

In the role of a cook carrying a goose in a basket
Terracotta statuette. H 145 mm
Mainland Greek, late 3rd – early 2nd centuries BC
Collection: Ricketts and Shannon (no. GR.85d.1937)
Exhibition: *Greek Art, 1903*, p. 85, no. 77, pl. LXXXIV
Literature: T. B. L. Webster, *Monuments Illustrating New Comedy*
(London 1961) p. 67

38 🐦 LITTLE GIRL SEATED

Terracotta statuette. H 87 mm
Attic, or Boeotian derived from Attic, c. 340–330 BC
Collection: Ricketts and Shannon (no. GR.86a.1937)
Exhibition: *Greek Art, 1903*, p. 75, no. 25, pl. LXXV

39 🐦 BOY WITH PURSE

Terracotta statuette. H 122 mm
Boeotian, 3rd century BC
Collection: Ricketts and Shannon (no. GR.84.1937)

40   YOUNG WOMAN

Terracotta statuette. H 135 mm
Attic or Boeotian, earlier 3rd century BC
Collection: Ricketts and Shannon (no. GR.77.1937)
Exhibition: *Greek Art, 1903*, p. 72, no. 20, pl. LXXV

41   THREE FLYING EROTES

Terracotta statuettes. H between 45 and 75 mm
Boeotian or Euboean, 3rd century BC
Collection: Ricketts and Shannon (no. GR.93a–c.1937)

42   FLYING EROS

Terracotta statuette. H 235 mm
Sicilian(?), from Magna Graecia, 2nd century BC
Collection: Ricketts and Shannon (no. GR.81.1937)
Exhibition: *Greek Art, 1903*, pp. 73–4, no. 17, pl. LXX

43   YOUNG WOMAN

Terracotta statuette. H 245 mm
Asia Minor, derived from Attic, 3rd century BC
Collection: Ricketts and Shannon (no. GR.68.1937)
Exhibition: *Greek Art, 1903*, p. 71, no. 2, pl. LXXIII

44   YOUNG WOMAN

Terracotta statuette. H 285 mm
Boeotian, 3rd century BC
Collection: Ricketts and Shannon (no. GR.64.1937)
Exhibition: *Greek Art, 1903*, p. 72, no. 5, pl. LXXIII

45   YOUNG WOMAN (see pl. 6)

Terracotta statuette. H 240 mm
Boeotian, 3rd century BC
Collection: Ricketts and Shannon (no. GR.62.1937)
Exhibition: *Greek Art, 1903*, p. 73, no. 15, pl. LXXVII

46 🐦 YOUNG WOMAN (see pl. 6)

Terracotta statuette. H 280 mm
Tarentine, 3rd century BC
Collection: Ricketts and Shannon (no. GR.63.1937)

47 🐦 YOUNG WOMAN

Terracotta statuette. H 275 mm
Asia Minor, 2nd century BC
Collection: Ricketts and Shannon (no. GR.65.1937)

48 🐦 YOUNG WOMAN

Terracotta statuette. H 255 mm
Asia Minor (Myrina), 2nd century BC
Collection: Ricketts and Shannon (no. GR.66.1937)

49 🐦 GOBLET (see pl. 7)

Pottery vase; stylised octopus. H 175 mm
Late Helladic IIIB, 13th century BC
Collection: Ricketts and Shannon (no. GR.41.1937)
Literature: *C.V.A. Cambridge* II pl. XVIII,1

50 🐦 THREE ALABASTRA (SCENT BOTTLES)

(a) Lions, siren. (b) Cocks, snake. (c) Boread
Pottery vases. (a) H 78 mm; (b) H 83 mm; (c) H 83 mm
Early Corinthian, *c.* 620–600 BC
Collection: Ricketts and Shannon ((a) no. GR.47.1937, (b) no. GR.45.1937, (c) no. GR.46.1937)
Literature: *C.V.A. Cambridge* II, pl. XVIII,5–7

51 🐦 LARGE ALABASTRON

Male and female sirens
Pottery vase. H 186 mm
End of Middle Corinthian, *c.* 580–570 BC
Collection: Ricketts and Shannon (no. GR.42.1937)
Literature: *C.V.A. Cambridge* II, pl. XVIII,2

52 🐉 TWO KYATHOI

(a) Dionysos banqueting, eyes, satyrs. (b) Dionysos and satyr, eyes, sphinxes; woman's moulded head under handle
Attic black-figure pottery. (a) H 153 mm; (b) H 150 mm
Group of Vatican G.57, *c.* 510–500 BC
Collection: Ricketts and Shannon (nos. GR.10.1937 and GR.9.1937)
Exhibition: (b) *Greek Art, 1903*, pp. 95–6, no. 7, pl. LXXXIX
Literature: (a) *C.V.A. Cambridge* II, pl. III,2; Beazley, *A.B.V.* p. 611, no. 15; (b) *C.V.A. Cambridge* II, pl. III,1; Beazley, *A.B.V.* no. 5

Dipper-shaped drinking vessels of Etruscan inspiration.

53 🐉 LEKYTHOS (OIL-FLASK)

Victory with a sash
Attic white-ground pottery. H 208 mm
In the manner of the Providence Painter, *c.* 460–450 BC
Collection: Ricketts and Shannon (no. GR.31.1937)
Literature: *C.V.A. Cambridge* II, pl. XIV,1; Beazley, *A.R.V.*, p. 1663

54 🐉 LEKYTHOS

Two women at the graveside, one of them mourning, the other bringing offerings
Attic white-ground pottery. Somewhat restored. H 275 mm
In the manner of the Bird Painter, *c.* 430–420 BC
Collection: Ricketts and Shannon (no. GR.33.1937)
Literature: *C.V.A. Cambridge* II, pl. XIV,3; Beazley, *A.R.V.*, p. 1234, no. 17

55 🐉 OINOCHOE (WINE-JUG)

Athena watching Herakles wrestling with the Nemean Lion
Attic black-figure pottery. H 256 mm
Class of the Red-Line Painter's oinochoai, and possibly exceptionally careful work by the Red-Line Painter himself, *c.* 500 BC
Collection: Ricketts and Shannon (no. GR.7.1937)
Literature: *C.V.A. Cambridge* II, pl. II,2; Beazley, *A.B.V.*, p. 607

56 ⥋ OINOCHOE

Hermes conducting Hera, Athena, and Aphrodite to Paris' adjudication
Attic black-figure pottery. H 290 mm
R.S. Class, by the Athena Painter, *c.* 500–490 BC
Collection: Ricketts and Shannon (no. GR.8.1937)
Literature: J. Millingen, *Peintures de vases antiques de la collection de Sir John Coghill, Bart.* (Rome 1817) pl. XXXIV,1; C. H. E. Haspels, *Attic Black-Figured Lekythoi* (Paris 1936) app. XV, no. 111; *C.V.A. Cambridge* II, p. 54 (where further bibliography), pl. II,3; Beazley, *A.B.V.*, p. 526, no. 1

57 ⥋ LEKYTHOS

Ariadne (?) mounting a chariot before Dionysos and a maenad; a satyr and a doe
Attic black-figure pottery. H 150 mm
By the Haimon Painter, *c.* 480 BC
Collection: Ricketts and Shannon (no. GR.48.1937)
Literature: C. H. E. Haspels, *Attic Black-Figured Lekythoi* (Paris 1936) app. XIII, no. 35; *C.V.A. Cambridge* II, pl. XVIII,9; Beazley, *A.B.V.*, p. 538

58 ⥋ LEKYTHOS

Fleeing woman
Attic red-figure pottery. H 369 mm
By the Berlin Painter, *c.* 470 BC
Collection: Ricketts and Shannon (no. GR.28.1937); formerly Giudice collection, Girgenti
Literature: J. D. Beazley, *Der Berliner Maler* (Berlin 1930) p. 20, no. 162; *C.V.A. Cambridge* II, pl. XIII,2; Beazley, *A.R.V.*, p. 211, no. 205

This vase illustrates the rather mannered style adopted by this artist, one of the greatest of late archaic vase-painters, in his last years.

59 ⥋ LEKYTHOS

Athena pouring a libation, attended by Victory
Attic red-figure pottery. Somewhat restored. H 345 mm
By the Achilles Painter, *c.* 460 BC
Collection: Ricketts and Shannon (no. GR.29.1937)

Exhibition: *Greek Art, 1903*, p. 107, no. 42, pl. xcv
Literature: *C.V.A. Cambridge* II, p. 59 (where further bibliography) pl. XIII,3; Beazley, *A.R.V.*, p. 993, no. 79

This lekythos shows the lingering archaism of the style employed by the Achilles Painter in his youth, as a pupil of the Berlin Painter.

60 ✤ LEKYTHOS

Hermes with a goddess (Hebe?) about to pour a libation
Attic red-figure pottery. H 418 mm
By the Achilles Painter, *c.* 450–440 BC
Collection: Ricketts and Shannon (no. GR.30.1937); bought from Amor in St James's Street
Exhibition: London, Goldsmiths' Hall *Treasures of Cambridge* (1959) no. 435
Literature: *C.V.A. Cambridge* II, pl. XIII,4; Beazley, *A.R.V.*, p. 993, no. 81

This lekythos aptly illustrates the stage in this artist's work when he emerges as probably the greatest of classical vase-painters.

61 ✤ ALABASTRON (SCENT BOTTLE)

Youth and two women
Attic red-figure pottery. H 125 mm
Paidikos Group, in the manner of the Euergides Painter, *c.* 510–500 BC
Collection: Ricketts and Shannon (no. GR.39.1937)
Literature: *C.V.A. Cambridge* II, pl. XVI,3; Beazley, *A.R.V.*, p. 100, no. 15

62 ✤ LEKYTHOS (OIL-FLASK)

Flying Eros playing the double flute
Attic red-figure pottery. H 282 mm
Class BL, by the Bowdoin Painter, *c.* 480–470 BC
Collection: Ricketts and Shannon (no. GR.27.1937)
Literature: *C.V.A. Cambridge* II, pl. XIII,1; A. Greifenhagen, *Griechische Eroten* (Berlin 1957) p. 15; Beazley, *A.R.V.*, p. 683, no. 123

63 🐍 HEAD-VASE (OINOCHOE)

Garlanded woman (maenad)
Attic moulded pottery. Handle restored. P H 183 mm (to rim)
Cook Class, *c.* 480–450 BC
Collection: Ricketts and Shannon (no. GR.38.1937)
Literature: *C.V.A. Cambridge* II, pl. XVI,2; Beazley, *A.R.V.*, p. 1540, no. 19

64 🐍 MUG-SHAPED OINOCHOE

Athlete with a strigil, his garments draped over a winning-post
Attic red-figure pottery. H 110 mm
By the Akestorides Painter, *c.* 460 BC
Collection: Ricketts and Shannon (no. GR.37.1937)
Literature: *C.V.A. Cambridge* II, pl. XVI,1; Beazley, *A.R.V.*, p. 782, no. 13

65 🐍 SMALL NECK-AMPHORA

Youth with a staff. Other side: woman spinning; inscribed 'the boy is beautiful', 'beautiful [girl]'
Attic red-figure pottery. H 309 mm
By the Triptolemos Painter, *c.* 480 BC
Collection: Ricketts and Shannon (no. GR.24.1937)
Literature: J. Millingen, *Peintures de vases antiques de la collection de Sir John Coghill, Bart.* (Rome 1817) pl. XXII,1; *C.V.A. Cambridge* II, p. 58 (where further bibliography) pls.XI,2, XVII,7,11; Beazley, *A.R.V.*, p. 362, no. 15, p. 1648

Such small amphorae seem to have served as decanters.

66 🐍 NECK-AMPHORA

Eos pursuing Tithonos, although the goddess has already taken the youth's lyre (!). Other side: Theseus about to kill Procrustes
Attic red-figure pottery. H 340 mm
By the Pig Painter, *c.* 480–470 BC
Collection: Ricketts and Shannon (no. GR.22.1937)
Literature: *C.V.A. Cambridge* II, pls. X,2, XVII,9–10; Beazley, *A.R.V.*, p. 565, no. 36; J. Boardman, *Athenian Red-Figure Vases: The Archaic Period* (London 1975) p. 180, fig. 319

37

67 🐟 SMALL NECK-AMPHORA

Ganymedes (with hoop) pursued by Zeus. Other side: old man
Attic red-figure pottery. H 286 mm
By the Briseis Painter, *c.* 470 BC
Collection: Ricketts and Shannon (no. GR.23.1937)
Exhibition: *Greek Art, 1903*, p. 103, no. 22, pl. XCII
Literature: *C.V.A. Cambridge* II, p. 58 (where further bibliography) pls.
XI,1, XVII,3,6,8; Beazley, *A.R.V.*, p. 409, no. 51

68 🐟 EYE-CUP

Interior: Gorgoneion. Exterior: between vines and eyes, Dionysos and
satyrs, Herakles and Kyknos
Attic black-figure pottery. H 155 mm, D 375 mm
Andokides Class, by the Lysippides Painter, *c.* 530–520 BC
Collection: Ricketts and Shannon (no. GR.12.1937)
Literature: *C.V.A. Cambridge* II, pls. IV,1, VIII,1, IX,4; H. Bloesch,
Formen attischer Schalen (Berne 1940) p. 13, no. 5, pl. IV,2; Beazley,
A.B.V., p. 257, no. 23

The shape is the ordinary Greek kylix, or wine-cup.

69 🐟 CUP

Interior: boy inside a bell-krater (bowl for mixing wine). Exterior:
between palmettes, young revellers and young athletes; inscribed 'The
boy, yes. The boy is beautiful'
Attic red-figure pottery. H 125 mm, D 340 mm
From Vulci, *c.* 510–500 BC
Collection: Ricketts and Shannon (no. GR.15.1937)
Literature: *Collection de M. E[vangelos Triantaphyllos], vente, Paris 2–4
juin 1904*, no. 248, pl. XI; *C.V.A. Cambridge* II, p. 55 (where further
bibliography) pls. V,2, VIII,4, IX,1; Beazley, *A.R.V.*, p. 91, no. 54; *Apollo*
LXXXIII (1966) p. 138, fig. 1

A missing fragment of this vase is in the Villa Giulia, Rome.

70  CUP (see pl. 8)

Interior: reveller with lyre. Exterior: youths banqueting, battle scene;
nonsense inscriptions
Attic red-figure pottery. H 110 mm, Diam 273 mm
Wider circle of the Nikosthenes Painter, *c.* 500–490 BC
Collection: Ricketts and Shannon (no. GR.19.1937); bought from
W. T. Ready; formerly Higgins collection
Exhibition: *Greek Art, 1903*, p. 121, no. 82, pl. XCVI
Literature: *C.V.A. Cambridge* II, pls. VII,2, VIII,6, IX,5; Beazley, *A.R.V.*,
p. 135, no. 13

71 🐦 PELIKE

Both sides: tipsy revellers returning home with music
Attic black-figure pottery of the Leagros Group. H 268 mm
In the manner of the Acheloos Painter, *c.* 510–500 BC
Collection: Ricketts and Shannon (no. GR.57.1937)
Literature: Beazley, *A.B.V.*, p. 386, no. 11

The pelike probably served as a form of decanter.

72 🐦 ONE-PIECE AMPHORA

Athena greeting a young warrior on his return home; youth welcomed
by his own family
Attic red-figure pottery. H 490 mm
By the Painter of Louvre G231, *c.* 470–460 BC
Collection: Ricketts and Shannon (no. GR.21.1937)
Literature: *C.V.A. Cambridge* II, pls. X,1, XVII,1–2,4–5; Beazley, *A.R.V.*,
p. 580, no. 2

73 🐦 PELIKE

Man pursuing a youth who is warding him off with his lyre; man and
boy talking
Attic red-figure pottery. H 357 mm
By the Aegisthus Painter, *c.* 470–460 BC
Collection: Ricketts and Shannon (no. GR.26.1937); bought from
Spink and Sons
Literature: *C.V.A. Cambridge* II, pl. XII,2; Beazley, *A.R.V.*, p. 506, no.
21; G. Neumann, *Gesten und Gebärden in der griechischen Kunst* (Berlin
1965) p. 109

74 🙟 WOMAN OR GODDESS HOLDING A GARLAND

Pentelic marble relief fragment. P H 663 mm
Attic, *c.* 340 BC
Collection: Ricketts and Shannon (no. GR.99.1937)
Literature: Budde and Nicholls, *Sculpture*, pp. 17–18, no. 37, pl. IX

The fragment apparently came from a monumental base with widely spaced relief figures. The back of the block was sawn away in modern times.

75 🙟 HEAD FROM A SPHINX

Luna marble. Nose restored. P H 254 mm
Roman copy of about Augustan date, after a lost Greek original of *c.* 460–450 BC
Collection: Ricketts and Shannon (no. GR.96.1937)
Literature: *American Journal of Archaeology* LXIII (1959) p. 143, no. 10; Budde and Nicholls, *Sculpture*, pp. 20–2, no. 41, pl. X

76 🙟 HEAD OF A YOUNG WOMAN

Proconnesian statuary (?) marble. Restorations of sidelocks removed and some recutting of hair. H 276 mm
Hellenistic, later 2nd century BC
Collection: Ricketts and Shannon (no. GR.95.1937)
Exhibition: London, Goldsmiths' Hall *Treasures of Cambridge* (1959) no. 458
Literature: C. Winter, *The Fitzwilliam Museum* (1958) no. 13 with pl. facing; *American Journal of Archaeology* LXIII (1959) p. 143, no. 26; Budde and Nicholls, *Sculpture*, p. 40, no. 69, pl. XXI; *Apollo* LXXIII (1966) p. 141, fig. 8

The head was carved for insertion on a draped statue.

77 🦎 TORSO OF APOLLO KILLING A LIZARD, AFTER PRAXITELES

Pentelic marble. P H 850 mm
Early Roman copy after a lost Greek original of *c.* 360–350 BC
Collection: Ricketts and Shannon (no. GR.94.1937)
Literature: J. Chittenden and C. Seltman, *Greek Art* (London 1946) p. 36, no. 154, pl. XLII; *American Journal of Archaeology* LXIII (1959) p. 143, no. 20; Budde and Nicholls, *Sculpture*, pp. 27–8, no. 51, pl. XV; *Vita d'Arte* XXVII (1910) p. 2 with text fig.

This outstandingly sensitive copy of a lost masterpiece appears in the background of the self-portrait of Charles Shannon painted in 1907 (cf. article in *Vita d'Arte* XXVII (1910) p. 2 with text fig.). The sculpture remains on display in the Greek Room; a photograph is shown in the exhibition.

78 🦎 THE LANSDOWNE HOUSE ANTINOUS

Luna marble. Nose, bust, and parts of garland restored. P H of ancient part 410 mm
Roman, AD 130–40
Collection: Ricketts and Shannon (no. GR.100.1937); acquired March 1930 (one of the last additions to the Ricketts and Shannon collection) at Christie's, Cat. 5 March 1930, p. 16, no. 18, p. 81
Literature: F. Poulsen, *Greek and Roman Portraits in English Country Houses* (Oxford 1923) p. 78, no. 63 with pl. facing; R. West, *Römische Porträtplastik* II (Munich 1941) p. 136, no. 2, pl. XXXVIII; Budde and Nicholls, *Sculpture*, pp. 68–9, no. 109 (where further bibliography) pl. XXXVI; C. W. Clairmont, *Die Bildnisse des Antinous* (Rome 1966) p. 56, no. 55

Found in 1769 in Hadrian's Villa at Tivoli, and acquired in 1772 by the Earl (later first Marquess) of Shelburne for Lansdowne House. It was probably originally set on an over-life-size statue showing the dead favourite of the Emperor Hadrian deified as the god Bacchus.

GEMS

79 🦎 SAPPHIRINE CHALCEDONY LENTOID

Cow and calf
Minoan, 14th century BC
Collection: Ricketts and Shannon (no. S.1   GR.118.1937)

80 🦎 GREEN JASPER SCARAB

Youth with lyre and cock
Graeco-Phoenician, *c.* 500 BC
Collection: Ricketts and Shannon (no. S.4)

81 🦎 ROCK CRYSTAL SCARAB

Dionysos holding a *kantharos* and an ivy stem
Greek, *c.* 500 BC. Modern ring
Collection: Ricketts and Shannon (no. S.5); formerly Wyndham Cook
collection

82 🦎 SARD SCARAB

Dancing satyr with double flute
Etruscan, earlier 5th century BC. Modern ring
Collection: Ricketts and Shannon (no. S.7)

83 🦎 CORNELIAN RING-STONE

Hermes, signed 'of Dioskourides'
Roman of the time of Augustus. Modern ring
Collection: Ricketts and Shannon (no. S.25); formerly collections of
Fulvio Orsini, Baron Stosch, and the Duke of Marlborough

Signed by Dioskourides, the greatest Roman gem-engraver.

84 🦎 OVAL CABOCHON GARNET

Kneeling satyr removing a thorn from the foot of another satyr
Italian, 16th century
Collection: Ricketts and Shannon (no. S.35)

85 🦎 TWO-LAYER ONYX CAMEO

Head of Medusa
Italian, 16th century
Collection: Ricketts and Shannon (no. S.38)

86 🐍 ENAMELLED FOB SEAL

Sard intaglio engraved with the figure of the *diskobolos*
Italian, early 17th century; engraving after the Greek sculptor, Myron
Collection: Ricketts and Shannon (no. S.32)

87 🐍 SARD INTAGLIO IN FOLDING GOLD RING

Warrior with his horse
English, 18th century
Collection: Ricketts and Shannon (no. S.20)

88 🐍 SARD INTAGLIO IN HEAVY GOLD RING

Head of Herakles
English, 18th century
Collection: Ricketts and Shannon (no. S.24)

EUROPEAN ART

89 🐍 LEON NIKOLAJEWITSCH BAKST
1866–1924 (see pl. 9)

La Princesse Aurore
Pencil, watercolour, with gold and silver paint heightened with white.
300 × 227 mm
Signed and dated lower right corner 'bakst 22'
Collection: Ricketts and Shannon (no. 1976)
Exhibitions: include Edinburgh Festival and London *The Diaghilev Exhibition* (1954) no. 290
Literature: R. Buckle, *In Search of Diaghilev* (1955) repr. pl. 99, p. 79;
C. Spencer, *Leon Bakst* (1973) repr. pl. 209

This is a design for the wedding dress of the Princesse Aurore in *The Sleeping Princess – Aurora's Wedding*, a ballet as performed in Paris in 1922 by the Diaghilev company.

Ricketts was enthusiastic about the Russian ballet and had a high opinion of Bakst's designs, which he described in a letter as a 'well-nigh perfect manifestation of beauty, enthusiasm and adventure'.

90   FEDERICO BAROCCI   1535–1612 (see pl. 10)

A study for Christ on the Cross with two angels
Black chalk, heightened with white on blue paper, squared for
enlargement and transfer. 515 × 410 mm
Inscribed verso in ink 'Del Barrocci'
Collection: Ricketts and Shannon (no. 1978)
Reference: *European Drawings from the Fitzwilliam* (1976–7) no. 2, pp.
3 and 4, pl. 2

A drawing for the altarpiece painted for the chapel of Count Pietro
Bonarelli in the Chiesa del Crocefisso Miracoloso at Urbino around
1566, now in the Galleria Nazionale delle Marche, Urbino.

91   FEDERICO BAROCCI   1535–1612

A study for the figure of the Virgin in a Nativity
Black and white chalk on buff paper, squared for transfer, laid down.
333 × 243 mm
Inscribed lower left 'f. Barocci'
Collection: Ricketts and Shannon (no. 1977)
Reference: *European Drawings from the Fitzwilliam* (1976–7) no. 4, pl.
4, pp. 4 and 5

One of a number of studies for the well-documented *Nativity* painted
for Barocci's patron Francesco Maria II della Rovere, Duke of Urbino,
paid for in 1597, and now in the Prado. The finished painting differs
considerably from this drawing, which however anticipates another
study in the Uffizi.

92   JACOPO BASSANO   1510–1592

Study of a manservant, seen from behind
Charcoal and black chalk, heightened with white. 192 × 162 mm
Inscribed in ink lower right 'Bassano'
Collection: Ricketts and Shannon (no. 1980)
Reference: *European Drawings from the Fitzwilliam* (1976–7) no. 6, pp.
5 and 6, pl. 6

This figure is a study for the servant on the right of *The Return of the
Prodigal Son*, known only from an engraving by Pietro Monaco (active
1707–*c.* 1775).

44

93 🦎 ANTONIO GALLI BIBIENA 1700–1774

Design for a stage scenery
Pen and ink and bistre wash. 308 × 354 mm
Collection: Ricketts and Shannon (no. 1982)
Exhibition: Magnasco Society *Exhibition of Drawings* (1927) no. 56, as
G. B. Bibiena

The attribution is tentative: W. G. Constable has suggested that this
drawing may be by a Venetian painter. This sort of drawing was of
particular interest to Ricketts as a point of reference for his stage designs.

94 🦎 FERNANDO GALLI BIBIENA 1657–1743

Palace interior with a double staircase
Pen and ink with grey and sepia wash. 256 × 270 mm
Collection: Ricketts and Shannon (no. 1985)
Exhibition: Magnasco Society *Exhibition of Drawings* (1927) no. 54, as
G. B. Bibiena

Another of the five drawings attributed to the Bibiena family from the
Ricketts and Shannon collection. This attribution is also tentative.

95 🦎 BRITISH SCHOOL *c.* 1595–1600

Unknown man
Oil on wood. 768 × 622 mm
Collection: Ricketts and Shannon (no. 2051); bought after 1922; came
earlier from Condover Hall, Shropshire, where the collection of
pictures had been chiefly formed by Nicholas Owen Smythe (d. 1814)
Literature: John Woodward, *A Picture History of British Painting* (1962)
p. 24; Roy Strong in *Apollo* LXXIX (1964) p. 269

The painting is dated from the costume. The man is probably a lover,
characteristically dressed in black, wearing a hat, arms folded in the pose
of an afflicted lover, his gaze fixed on some vision of delight. The scene,
despite discrepancies, appears to be intended for London.

96 🦎 SIR EDWARD COLEY BURNE-JONES
1833–1898

The Backgammon Players
Black chalk with some body colour. 602 × 1029 mm
Signed with a monogram and dated lower right-hand corner 'EBJ 1861'
Collection: Ricketts and Shannon (no. 2004); owned by Charles Fairfax
Murray, 1904
Exhibitions: Tate Gallery *Burne-Jones* (1933) no. 191; Arts Council
Burne-Jones (1975) no. 31

This large and proficient drawing reflects the idyllic, medievalised
atmosphere of William Morris' Red House, whose garden is the model
for the setting. The girl is a likeness of Jane Morris. A small watercolour
version is at Birmingham, dating from 1862, and a similar design is on
a painted cabinet in the Metropolitan Museum, New York.

97 🦎 SIR EDWARD COLEY BURNE-JONES
1833–1898

Study for *The Passing of Venus*
Pencil on green paper. 252 × 156 mm
Collection: Ricketts and Shannon·(no. 2015.1); bought at Christie's, 5
June 1919
Exhibitions: include Tate Gallery *Burne-Jones* (1933)
Literature: Harrison and Waters, *Burne-Jones* (1973) pl. 26

The Passing of Venus was originally a design for tiles (1861) but was later
used in the background of *Laus Veneris* (1875) and for two oil paintings,
at Exeter College Oxford (1876) and an unfinished version in the Tate
Gallery.

98 🦎 SIR EDWARD COLEY BURNE-JONES
1833–1898

Seven studies of drapery for the angels in *The Days of Creation*
Pencil. (1) 230 × 105 mm; (2) 230 × 102 mm; (3) 230 × 83 mm; (4)
230 × 94 mm; (5) 230 × 100 mm; (6) 230 × 90 mm; (7) 230 × 105 mm
Each signed 'E.B.J. 1872'; (7) also 'studies of drapery for Angels of
Creation' (signed lower right-hand corner, except (1) and (6) lower left
corner)
Collection: Ricketts and Shannon (nos. 2013.1–7); bought at Christie's,
5 June 1919

Literature: Harrison and Waters, *Burne-Jones* (1973) pp. 110 and 113;
A. C. Sewter, *The Stained Glass of William Morris and his Circle* (1975)
I, pl. 322, II, p. 147

The Days of Creation (1872–6) is in the Fogg Art Museum, Harvard
University. The design originated in a set of small tracery angels at
Middleton Cheney, Northamptonshire – the glass of which dates from
1870.

99   SIR EDWARD COLEY BURNE-JONES
        1833–1898

Study for *The Mirror of Venus*
Pencil. 224 × 174 mm
Collection: Ricketts and Shannon (no. 2003.4); bought at Christie's, 5
June 1919

This study for the reflection of the central kneeling girl, and a detail
of a hand, may be dated 1873, the year in which the artist started on
his large oil version of the subject. A reflected image is a device used
in several of Shannon's portraits.

100   SIR EDWARD COLEY BURNE-JONES
        1833–1898

Study for the head of a girl in *The Passing of Venus*
Pencil and highlights in white body colour on green paper. 210 × 174
mm
Collection: Ricketts and Shannon (no. 2017); bought at Christie's,
5 June 1919
Exhibitions: include Tate Gallery *Burne-Jones* (1933)
Literature; Harrison and Waters, *Burne-Jones* (1973) pl. 26

A highly finished drawing of the head of a girl. The quality of this sort
of drawing was something Ricketts regretted that he himself could not
achieve – 'My painting refuses to face detail and certain kinds of
invention, which Moreau or Burne-Jones have at their finger-tips.'

101 🖎 SIR EDWARD COLEY BURNE-JONES
1833–1898

Studies for *The Days of Creation*
Pencil on white cartridge paper. 362 × 245 mm
Signed lower right-hand corner 'EBJ 1876. Studies for the DAYS OF CREATION'
Collection: Ricketts and Shannon (no. 1995); bought at Christie's, 5 June 1919

A study of hands and drapery, with the face and wings of an angel holding the globe roughly sketched in, and a study of drapery for the torso of an angel. The painting is in the Fogg Art Museum, Harvard University.

102 🖎 SIR EDWARD COLEY BURNE-JONES
1833–1898 (see pl. 11)

Study for the figure of a Gorgon in the *Perseus* series
Pencil. 271 × 178 mm
Signed and dated lower right-hand corner 'EBJ 1876'
Collection: Ricketts and Shannon (no. 2020); bought at Christie's, 5 June 1919
Literature: Kurt Löcher, *Der Perseus Zyklus* (1973) p. 62 and cat.

A study for the right-hand Gorgon in *The Finding of Medusa* from the Perseus series. A study for the same figure is at Birmingham.

103 🖎 SIR EDWARD COLEY BURNE-JONES
1833–1898

Study for *The Annunciation*
Pencil. 273 × 180 mm
Inscribed 'Virgin's feet Annunciation'; not the artist's writing
Collection: Ricketts and Shannon (no. 2010.4); bought at Christie's, 5 June 1919

This study is for the feet of the Virgin in *The Annunciation* (1876–9) at the Lady Lever Art Gallery, Port Sunlight, of which the cartoon is at Norwich Castle Museum.

    More than eighty drawings by Burne-Jones were bequeathed to the Fitzwilliam Museum by the artists.

48

104 SIR EDWARD COLEY BURNE-JONES
1833–1898

Study of drapery
Pencil. 179 × 227 mm
Collection: Ricketts and Shannon (no. 2014.2); bought at Christie's,
5 June 1919
Literature: M. I. Wilson, 'The Case of the Victorian Piano' in *V & A
Yearbook 3* (1972) pp. 133–50; M. I. Wilson, 'Burne-Jones and Piano
Reform', *Apollo* CII (1975) p. 346

This study is for the figure of a poet painted on the upper lid of the
'Graham Piano' (1880).

105 SIR EDWARD COLEY BURNE-JONES
1833–1898

Study for *The Golden Stairs*
Pencil. 253 × 176 mm
Collection: Ricketts and Shannon (no. 2010.2); bought at Christie's,
5 June 1919

This drawing of hands and musical instruments is for the picture in the
Tate Gallery of 1880.

106 SIR EDWARD COLEY BURNE-JONES
1833–1898

Portrait study of a lady
Black chalk. 322 × 230 mm
Signed 'EBJ 1889'
Collection: Ricketts and Shannon (no. 2018)

The sitter may be Helen Mary Gaskell, a friend of the artist.

107 ERNEST COLE b. 1890

Sheet of studies: heads and figures
Red chalk. 247 × 305 mm
Collection: Ricketts and Shannon (no. 2027.9)

The Michelangelesque quality of Cole's drawings attracted Ricketts when Cole was still a student. His subsequent career as a modern sculptor was a bitter disappointment, since he renounced the classic European tradition that Ricketts and Shannon revered.

108 ✍ ERNEST COLE b. 1890

Sheet of male nude studies
Red chalk. 422 × 279 mm
Collection: Ricketts and Shannon (no. 2027.13)

Cole was responsible for the sculptural decoration on the façade of County Hall, London, with which some of the thirty-four drawings by him in the Fitzwilliam Museum are connected. Ricketts made an unsuccessful attempt to get Cole exemption from military service in the First World War because of his outstanding artistic ability – 'an artist', wrote Ricketts, 'whom I compare to Alfred Stevens, and whose loss in the trenches I would consider a national disaster'.

109 ✍ JAN COSSIERS 1600–1671

Study of a head of a young man, looking up
Black, red, and white chalk. Top corners of the sheet cut off diagonally. 223 × 193 mm
Inscribed verso in pencil 'P P Rubens' and in ink 'F No. 3; 17'
Collection: Ricketts and Shannon (no. 2183)
Reference: *European Drawings from the Fitzwilliam* (1976–7) no. 64, p. 40, pl. 64

The attribution to Cossiers was first made by Michael Jaffé.

110 ✍ WALTER CRANE 1845–1915

The Death of the Year
Watercolour. 160 × 360 mm
Collection: Ricketts and Shannon (no. 2102)

This study was formerly attributed to Leighton, and appears as such in R. and L. Ormond, *Frederick Leighton* (1976). It was identified by Bill Waters as a drawing mentioned by Crane in his memoirs as being done in Rome during the winter of 1872–3 as an illustration for Shelley's poem. Crane's patron Somerset Beaumont commissioned a painting of a similar subject, *The Advent of Spring*.

111 🦎 LORENZO DI CREDI 1459–1537

Head of a youth looking up
Silverpoint heightened with white on buff-toned paper. 199 × 148 mm
Inscribed verso 'gio belieno'
Collection: Ricketts and Shannon (no. 2114); bought at the sale of Sir
J. C. Robinson, Christie's, 12 May 1902 (96)
Exhibitions: include Fitzwilliam Museum *15th- and 16th-Century Drawings* (1960) no. 23

The drawing is related in style to the head of a youth at Christ Church
Oxford datable 1480–5, and other Credi drawings at the British
Museum, at the Louvre, and in Bayonne. The Fitzwilliam drawing was
listed by Berenson in 1938, no. 670D.

Ricketts wrote after the sale, 'I secured one of the marvellous Credi
heads for £44.'

112 🦎 EUGÈNE DELACROIX 1798–1863 (see pl. 12)

Study for part of the 'Justice' frieze, Palais Bourbon
Oil on canvas. 387 × 610 mm
Collection: Ricketts and Shannon (no. 2033); bought by Shannon at
Christie's, 1–3 July 1897 (233)
Reference: Fitzwilliam Museum, *Catalogue of Paintings* I (1960) pp. 162
and 163, repr. pl. 88

An early stage in the designs for decorations of the Salon du Roi in the
Palais Bourbon (Chambre des Députés), Paris. The subjects of the
decorations are 'Justice', 'Agriculture', 'Industry', and 'War'. This
painting is the second part of the 'Justice' frieze, representing the
executive powers of the law. The design is close to a series of outline
and watercolour drawings of the whole scheme.

113 🦎 EUGÈNE DELACROIX 1798–1863

The Muse of Orpheus
Pen and ink heightened with oil paint; paper laid down on canvas,
hexagonal. 212 × 254 mm
Collection: Ricketts and Shannon (no. 2035); bought at Lord Leighton's
sale, Christie's, 11, 13 and 14 July 1896 (312)
Reference: Fitzwilliam Museum, *Catalogue of Paintings* I (1960) pp. 164
and 165, repr. pl. 88

This study is for one of the four pendentives in the library of the Palais du Luxembourg (Sénat), Paris. The subjects are Philosophy, Eloquence, Poetry, and Science – *The Muse of Orpheus* represents Poetry. The final picture differs from this study only in one major respect: the addition of some leaves of a book beside the left arm.

114 EUGÈNE DELACROIX 1798–1863

Ceres
Oil on canvas. 197 × 375 mm
Collection: Ricketts and Shannon (no. 2034); bought by Shannon at Christie's, 1–3 July 1897 (234)
Reference: Fitzwilliam Museum, *Catalogue of Paintings* I (1960) pp. 163 and 164, repr. pl. 88

A study for one of the ceiling panels in the Salon de la Paix in the old Hôtel de Ville, Paris, carried out between 1849 and 1853 and destroyed in 1871 during the Commune when the building was burnt. The subject was one of eight deities surrounding a circular painting containing an allegory of Peace. The design of *Ceres* and the motif of the date-palm go back to decorations for *Autumn* and *Summer* painted in the 1820s.

115 EUGÈNE DELACROIX 1798–1863

Study for Tam O'Shanter
Black lead on thin paper. 175 × 223 mm
Collection: Ricketts and Shannon (no. 2032B); originally from the collection of the artist
Reference: *European Drawings from the Fitzwilliam* (1976–7) no. 103, p. 65

The artist is known to have painted two versions of this subject, taken from a poem by Robert Burns. The location of neither painting is known, but they were done between 1825 and 1827: this drawing might be for either picture.

116 EUGÈNE DELACROIX 1798–1863 (see pl. 13)

Study of bathing women
Pen and brown ink, and black chalk. 252 × 392 mm
Inscribed in pencil, by the artist, 'les nus compelle d'oublier les maux de la vie, d'autre avec regret' (?), and verso, in another writing, 'D'

Collection: Ricketts and Shannon (no. 2031B); originally from the collection of the artist
Reference: *Cent dessins français du Fitzwilliam Museum* (1976) no. 21

The inscription is obscure, but the composition is possibly connected with *Femmes Turques au Bain* of 1854 at Wadsworth Atheneum, Hartford, Connecticut.

Bathers are a recurrent theme of Shannon's paintings and lithographs.

117 🪶 EUGÈNE DELACROIX 1798–1863

Studies for *Michelangelo in his Studio*
Black lead. 374 × 241 mm
Inscribed, by the artist, at top 'Le penseroso', 'les marbres gigantesques – la figure / de Michelange relativement / petite', and lower 'livre', 'Pinceaux', 'plans d'architectures / cartons'
Collection: Ricketts and Shannon (no. 2032D); originally from the collection of the artist
Exhibitions: Edinburgh and London, Arts Council *Delacroix* (1964) no. 167, repr. pl. 79; *Cent dessins français du Fitzwilliam Museum* (1976) no. 23

The drawing, and its companion in the Fitzwilliam (2032E), is a study for the painting in the Musée Fabre, Montpellier, begun in 1849 but not completed until 1853. Lee Johnson suggests that the statues in the background may inaccurately represent *Lorenzo de'Medici* and .the *Medici Madonna*.

118 🪶 EUGÈNE DELACROIX 1798–1863

Study for a ceiling(?) design
Pencil. 215 × 272 mm
Collection: Ricketts and Shannon (no. 2032 C); originally from the collection of the artist

The composition has not been identified.

119 🦎 EUGÈNE DELACROIX 1798–1863

Studies of a figure laid in a tomb
Black lead. 270 × 317 mm
Inscribed, by the artist, at top left 'voir Cymbeline', at bottom 'bon',
and verso 'A'
Collection: Ricketts and Shannon (no. 2032 G)

Despite the inscription, there is no evident connection with *Cymbeline*,
Act IV, and the subject may be an Entombment of Christ.

120 🦎 LOUIS FÉLIX DELARUE 1731–1777

Bacchanale
Red chalk. 402 × 531 mm
Inscribed indistinctly and dated lower left in red chalk '. . .f. Roma 1761'
(artist's name smudged by a stroke of red chalk), and verso in black chalk
'10 / Vente Moenet 8 Fevrier 32'
Collection: Ricketts and Shannon (no. 2056)
Reference: *Cent dessins français du Fitzwilliam Museum* (1976) no. 31

The attribution to Delarue has been convincingly made by Alain

Latreille. The composition is identical with a signed drawing of the same
composition in the Musée d'Orléans. The drawing was previously
attributed to Fragonard, and is probably one of two Fragonard sketches
Ricketts recorded as having bought in October 1916. At that time
'French drawings are a drug, no Frenchmen buying'.

121 🦎 ALBRECHT DÜRER 1471–1528

A river landscape
Silverpoint on prepared paper, reinforced with the pen. 145 × 206 mm
Signed at top centre with monogram 'AD' (probably a later addition);
inscribed verso in ink 'Samuel de Festetits Aº 1851', and in pencil 'foss'
and 'd'albert Dürer'
Collection: Ricketts and Shannon (no. 2042)
Literature: includes Fitzwilliam Museum, *15th- and 16th-Century Draw-
ings* (1960) no. 6

The drawing has generally been dated *c.* 1515–20, but it is not
universally accepted as by Dürer. It probably is by Dürer but has been
retouched and reworked by a later or perhaps contemporary hand. The
scene may be on the Middle Rhine, or on Lake Constance or Lake
Zurich.

122 🖎 SIR ANTHONY VAN DYCK 1599–1641 (see pl. 14)

Archbishop Laud
Oil on canvas. 1216 × 971 mm
Collection: Ricketts and Shannon (no. 2043)
Reference: Fitzwilliam Museum, *Catalogue of Paintings* I (1960) pp. 37 and 38, repr. pl. 18

Ricketts believed this to be the original portrait – not, as is now generally thought, the example at Leningrad. This painting is now regarded as a contemporary studio repetition.

William Laud (1573–1645) was appointed Archbishop of Canterbury in 1633; he was impeached by Parliament, and beheaded in 1645.

The painting was in a sale at Christie's on 30 January 1920. Afterwards, Ricketts wrote, 'We have had a great stroke of luck. We bought at Christie's (all London having seen it), at the price of a good frame, Van Dyck's missing portrait of Archbishop Laud.'

123 🖎 SIR ANTHONY VAN DYCK 1599–1641

Drapery study of a kneeling figure
Black chalk on buff paper heightened with white. 354 × 287 mm
Inscribed on the mount in pencil 'P P Rubens / Study of a stooping figure' and 'Van Dyck'.
Collection: Ricketts and Shannon (no. 2048)

Michael Jaffé suggests that this drawing is a study from life, and should be dated *c.* 1620.

124 🖎 WILLIAM ETTY 1787–1849

Two male nude studies
Oil on paper backed on canvas. 536 × 622 mm
Collection: Ricketts and Shannon (no. 2052); bought by Ricketts at Christie's, 16 July 1904 (27)
Literature: Dennis Far, *William Etty* (1958) p. 173, no. 206; Fitzwilliam Museum, *Catalogue of Paintings* III (1977) p. 72

This life study was probably made in the Royal Academy schools, where Etty worked throughout his career. It has been dated *c.* 1818–20.

125 🙢 DOMENICO FETTI 1589–c. 1624 (see pl. 15)

Figure with a donkey by a tree
Brush with red wash on red-toned paper, some red chalk. 190 × 126 mm
Inscriptions on the old mount attributing the drawing to Fetti, including the note that one handwriting was that of 'Sir Uvedale' (presumably Sir Uvedale Price)
Collection: Ricketts and Shannon (no. 2053)

The style is Venetian and painterly and corresponds to Fetti's late style. He was in Venice from 1621 until his death.

126 🙢 FLORENTINE SCHOOL Early 15th century

Virgin and Child
Tempera on wood. 845 × 432 mm
Collection: Ricketts and Shannon (no. 1987)
Reference: Fitzwilliam Museum, *Catalogue of Paintings* II (1967) pp. 54 and 55

Ricketts held this painting to be by Bicci di Lorenzo (Florentine, 1375–1452), but the condition of the picture (the faces strengthened, the Virgin's dress repainted) makes attribution problematic.

127 🙢 FRENCH SCHOOL c. 1575–1600

Scene from the Commedia dell'Arte
Bistre, pen, and wash. 260 × 362 mm
Collection: Ricketts and Shannon (no. 2259)
Literature: D. Ternois, *L'art de Jacques Callot* (1962) p. 234, pl. 13

Pantaloon and an *inamorato* in the centre of a stage, with an architectural backdrop. Ternois cites a drawing from the Cabinet des Estampes as by the same anonymous hand.

This is a subject with a special appeal for Ricketts, who replied to a suggestion from George Bernard Shaw that they should do a pantomime, 'I adore all pantomimes! Harlequin is Hermes, Proteus, Loki; Sganarelle, and Il Dottore are friends. Pantaloon represents all one's Uncles; if you write a pantomime I am very much your man – I would give very much to be able to see a *Commedia del Arte* or an old Roman farce.'

128 ❧   HENRY FUSELI   1741–1825 (see pl. 16)

Nude female figure, back view
Pencil and watercolours. 343 × 253 mm
Collection: Ricketts and Shannon (no. 2062)
Exhibition: Royal Academy *Age of Neoclassicism* (1972) no. 598
Literature: Gert Schiff, *Johann Heinrich Füssli* (1973) pl. 1457 where a
date of 1805–10 is proposed

129 ❧   NICCOLÒ DI PIETRO GERINI   active by
               1368, d. before 1416 (see pl. 17)

Virgin and Child
Tempera on wood. 1127 × 553 mm
Collection: Ricketts and Shannon (no. 2078)
Reference: Fitzwilliam Museum, *Catalogue of Paintings* II (1967) pp. 59
and 60

This painting was ascribed by Ricketts to Jacopo di Cione (mentioned
1368–94) but has affinities to a *Virgin and Child* at Boston, dated 1392.
The present attribution was made by Berenson in the 1930s.

130 ❧   FRANCISCO DE GOYA Y LUCIENTES
               1746–1828 (see pl. 18)

'Comico descubrimiento'
Black chalk or lithographic crayon on grey/white paper. 192 × 149 mm
Inscribed, by the artist, 'Comico descubrimiento' and top right corner
'51'
Collection: Ricketts and Shannon (no. 2066)
Exhibitions: include Royal Academy *Goya and his Times* (1963–4) no.
198

The title is 'comical discovery': a mass of grotesque human heads fill
a pit in which they are revealed as if by a sudden light or the withdrawal
of a cloth. The subject may refer to beheadings that took place during
the persecution of Spanish liberals after 1823, or alternatively the figures
may be the damned in Hell. The drawing has been dated 1824–5.

131 🦎 FRANCISCO DE GOYA Y LUCIENTES
1746–1828

'The pen is mightier than the sword'
Black chalk or lithographic crayon. 192 × 156 mm
Numbered by the artist '7' altered from '6', and verso 'Goya'
Collection: Ricketts and Shannon (no. 2068)
Reference: *European Drawings from the Fitzwilliam* (1976–7) no. 123, p. 77, pl. 123

The three drawings by Goya owned by Ricketts and Shannon belong to a series made in the last years of the artist's life in Bordeaux. This drawing has been dated *c.* 1825–6

Ricketts wrote of Goya, 'It is by his power of design – an original, varied and nervous form of design – that he excels even more than by his vivacity of workmanship and his marvellous if unequal gift of expression.'

132 🦎 FRANCISCO DE GOYA Y LUCIENTES
1746–1828 (see pl. 19)

'Segura union natural'
Black chalk on grey/white paper. 192 × 150 mm
Inscribed, by the artist, 'segura union ñatural' over earlier titles, one of which may read 'Hombre la mitad muger la otre' (half a man, the other [half] a woman); numbered '15' and 'Goya' (verso)
Collection: Ricketts and Shannon (no. 2067)
Exhibitions: include Royal Academy *Goya and his Times* (1963–4) no. 191

'Union secured by nature' is a light-hearted comment on the indissoluble bond of marriage.

133 🦎 FRANCESCO GUARDI   1712–1793

View of the Basin of St Mark, with San Giorgio Maggiore
Pen and dark brown ink. 168 × 244 mm
Collection: Ricketts and Shannon (no. 2070)

An extreme example of the artist's style. This view does not include the Campanile, either from choice or because it was being rebuilt: the former campanile fell down in 1774 and rebuilding was finished in 1791.

134 🦎 EGBERT VAN HEEMSKERK *c.* 1645–1704

Singing peasants
Oil on wood. 165 × 229 mm
Collection: Ricketts and Shannon (no. 1990)
Reference: Fitzwilliam Museum, *Catalogue of Paintings* I (1960) pp. 59
and 60

The former attribution of the painting was to Adrian Brouwer.

135 🦎 WILLIAM HOGARTH 1697–1764

Interior of the chapel of the Foundling Hospital
Pen and grey wash. 27 × 51 mm
Collection: Ricketts and Shannon (no. 2071)

The fact that the letters 'IHS' on the hanging of the pulpit are in reverse
suggests that the drawing was made for engraving.

136 🦎 WENZEL HOLLAR 1607–1677

A view of Struden on the Danube
Pen and brown ink, blue-grey and brown wash. 57 × 168 mm
Inscribed, by the artist, in ink lower centre 'Danubius', top centre
'Strudl'; on verso in ink 'N 26' and in pencil 'Wenceslaus Hollar'
Collection: Ricketts and Shannon (no. 2072)
Literature: Francis Springell, *Connoisseur and Diplomat* (1963) pp. 66,
114–15, n. 99, cat. no. LXXXV, pl. 41

The view depicts the rock island of Wörth, with a crucifix and the ruins
of the Castle of Werfenstein in the distance.

137 🦎 WOLFGANG HUBER *c.* 1480–1553

Crucifixion
Pen and indian ink. 320 × 215 mm
Collection: Ricketts and Shannon (no. 2076)
Reference: *European Drawings from the Fitzwilliam* (1976–7) no. 55

The drawing has been dated *c.* 1525. It may be connected with a lost
altarpiece which Huber painted in Passau during the 1520s.

138 🐦 WILLIAM HOLMAN HUNT 1827–1910

Claudio and Isabella
Pencil, pen and indian ink, and wash. 317 × 184 mm
Signed and dated bottom left with monogram 'WHH 1850'
Collection: Ricketts and Shannon (no. 2073), by 1907

A drawing illustrating *Measure for Measure*, Act III, scene i, and preliminary to the Tate Gallery picture of 1850. A letter by the artist stated, 'There were two original studies by me for Claudio and Isabella, one about 9 inches by 5, an elaborate pen and ink representing Claudio as in the picture, and Isabella with her back more turned round, her arms round her neck. Messrs Shannon and Ricketts I believe bought this from Exn in Leicester Galleries for £100...' Ricketts wrote on the mount that W. Deverell sat for Claudio.

139 🐦 JACOB JORDAENS 1593–1678

The head of a rider, mauled by a lion, after Sir Peter Paul Rubens
Black and red chalks heightened with white chalk. 220 × 246 mm
Collection: Ricketts and Shannon (no. 2184)

The drawing was believed by Ricketts and Shannon to be a study by Rubens himself. The head is copied from that of the rider being mauled by a lion at the centre of the *Lion and Leopard Hunt* which was painted to a design of Rubens by members of his workshop *c*. 1617. The picture (canvas, 2300 × 3170 mm) is now in Dresden (*Klassiker der Kunst* (1921 edn) 113). The combination of technique *en trois crayons*, the style and the rhythm in the morphology of features and muscling, as Michael Jaffé has pointed out, identify Jordaens as the draughtsman.

140 🐦 JACOB JORDAENS 1593–1678

Old man drinking (Portrait of Adam van Noort)
Red and black chalk heightened with white. Repairs to the sheet bottom left and right. 187 × 136 mm
Collection: Ricketts and Shannon (no. 2083)
Reference: *European Drawings from the Fitzwilliam* (1976–7) no. 75, p. 47, pl. 75

This study is for the king in *The King Drinks* (*c*. 1638–9) in the Musée des Beaux-Arts, Brussels. Adam van Noort (1557–1641) was the artist's father-in-law and former teacher.

60

141  JACOB JORDAENS 1593–1678

Design for a tapestry: a group of figures making music in an
architectural setting
Black and red chalk, pen and brown ink, grey and brown wash.
199 × 255 mm
Collection: Ricketts and Shannon (no. 2054)
Exhibitions: include Ottawa, National Gallery of Canada *Jordaens*
(1968) no. 204

Listed in the collection as by Erasmus Quellinus (1607–1678) but
accepted by several authorities as certainly by Jordaens. Michael Jaffé
suggests that the drawing may relate to a large decoration *A Balcony
with a Moor and a Woman*, in the artist's sale, the Hague, 22 March 1734,
no. 104, and that the drawing was for a wall decoration painted in
tempera on linen, not a tapestry.

142 ASCRIBED TO JACOB JORDAENS
1593–1678

Head of an old woman with spectacles
Black and red chalk, heightened with white. 169 × 123 mm
Collection: Ricketts and Shannon (no. 2082)

Probably a study for the head of an old woman seen on the left in *Christ
driving the money-changers from the Temple*, in the Louvre; but the
attribution is not entirely certain.

143 JACOB JORDAENS 1593–1678 (see pl. 20)

Diana and her nymphs returning from the chase (after Rubens)
Black and red chalk, brush, brown wash, and body colour. 347 × 408
mm
Verso: copies after other Rubens compositions
Collection: Ricketts and Shannon (no. 2235)
Reference: *European Drawings from the Fitzwilliam* (1976–7) no. 76

The present attribution to Jordaens is by Michael Jaffé: in the list of the
bequest it had been given to Theodor van Thulden (1606–1676).

61

144 CHARLES SAMUEL KEENE 1823–1891

Signs of Wet
Pen and brown ink, brown wash, and watercolour. 171 × 252 mm
Signed in ink at left 'C.K.', verso in pencil 'Drawing for Punch.
Longshoreman', on mount 'Charles Keene / Signs of Wet'
Collection: Ricketts and Shannon (no. 2086)

145 CHARLES SAMUEL KEENE 1823–1891

Sketch of a hunter
Pen and ink. 158 × 133 mm
Inscribed verso in pencil 'Drawing by Charles Keene, Henry Keene
collection'
Collection: Ricketts and Shannon (no. 2087)

Possibly a drawing for *Robinson Crusoe*. Keene was one of the illustrators
admired by Ricketts and Shannon in their early days, and an exemplar
for their black-and-white work.

146 NICHOLAS LANCRET 1690–1743

Study of a woman reclining
Sanguine. 132 × 112 mm
Collection: Ricketts and Shannon (no. 2094)
Reference: *Cent dessins français du Fitzwilliam Museum* (1976) no. 55

Listed in the collection as by Watteau, but rightly given to Lancret by
Parker in 1935. The figure is a study for a woman fishing in the painting
Water, one of a series of four depicting the elements formerly
belonging to the Marquis de Béringhen.

147 NICHOLAS LANCRET 1690–1743

Study of a seated lady: half-length, with the right hand at chin
Sanguine. 107 × 95 mm
Collection: Ricketts and Shannon (no. 2093)
Reference: *Cente dessins français du Fitzwilliam Museum* (1976) no. 54

Listed in the collection as by Watteau, but rightly given to Lancret by
Parker in 1935. The figure is a study for a painting *Le Jeu de Colin-Maillard*
(au Jardin) formerly in the Château de Sans-Souci in Potsdam.

148  ALPHONSE LEGROS 1837–1911

Death, the Wooer
Pencil, brush and sepia. 248 × 203 mm
Collection: Ricketts and Shannon (no. 2097)

The composition was engraved by Ricketts. The date of the drawing
is *c.* 1895, but it did not enter the possession of Ricketts and Shannon
before 1922.

149 JOHN FREDERICK LEWIS 1805–1876

Procida
Black chalk and watercolour, heightened with white on buff paper laid
down on mount. 257 × 351 mm
Inscribed and dated in pencil lower right 'Procida Aug 28'
Collection: Ricketts and Shannon (no. 2110); bought by Shannon at
Sotheby's, 4 November 1920 (409)
Exhibition: Guildford, Guildford House Gallery *J. F. Lewis: Painter of
the Desert and Harem* (1977) no. 62

The drawing may have been done at the same time as a sketch of Procida
in the Ashmolean Museum, Oxford, which is dated 29 August 1838.

150 JOHN FREDERICK LEWIS 1805–1876

The Siesta
Watercolour and body colour on paper, folded round a wooden panel.
Painted area 465 × 591 mm
Collection: Ricketts and Shannon (no. 2111)
Exhibition: Guildford, Guildford House Gallery *J. F. Lewis: Painter of
the Desert and Harem* (1977) no. 111

The drawing may be a study for *Siesta* of 1876 (Tate Gallery).

151 FRA FILIPPO LIPPI *c.* 1406–1469

Study of drapery with a bare arm
Silverpoint on grey-brown prepared paper. 191 × 213 mm
Verso: Black chalk, sketch of a coat of arms with an animal tied to a
column as a charge
Collection: Ricketts and Shannon (no. 2112)

152   BERNARDINO LUINI   1465/75–1533

Study for a Crucifixion
Red chalk. Paper relaid and repaired in several places. 254 × 183 mm
Inscribed in ink 'No 190'
Collection: Ricketts and Shannon (no. 2116)
Literature: Rosalda Gilardi Bernocco, 'La Crocefissione del Luini in Santa Maria degli Angeli a Lugano', *L'Arte* LVIII (October–December 1959) pp. 337 and 356, suggesting that this may be a sketch for the fresco discussed

153   ADOLF VON MENZEL   1815–1905

Study of a lady's head and hands
Black chalk or pencil. 134 × 210 mm
Collection: Ricketts and Shannon (no. 2118), by 1917

This is one of the drawings by an illustrator which shows the two artists' professional preferences. In Ricketts' view Menzel 'expresses profoundly that somewhat middleclass assertion of a busy, personal choice which finds a counterpart in the realistic literature of thirty years ago…no gallery of art which should aim at a comprehensive record of the nineteenth century could afford to be without some specimen of his work as a painter, and above all as a draughtsman'.

154   SIR JOHN EVERETT MILLAIS   1829–1896 (see pl. 21)

Christ in the house of his parents
Pencil. 196 × 337 mm
Signed lower left with monogram 'JEM'
Collection: Ricketts and Shannon (no. 2120); passed to Ricketts by S. C. Cockerell in 1911

A preliminary study for the painting exhibited at the Royal Academy in 1850, with variations. There are at least three related studies.

It is characteristic that the collection contained early drawings by Millais. Ricketts missed the early intensity of the Pre-Raphaelite work in Millais's later art – 'with John Everett Millais the public created an artist in its own image'.

155 🦎 SIR JOHN EVERETT MILLAIS 1829–1896 (see pl. 22)

Death and the lovers
Pen and brown ink, brown wash over pencil. 178 × 209 mm sheet, 167 × 194 mm within margin
Inscribed bottom right 'J. E. Millais'
Collection: Ricketts and Shannon (no. 2121)

The subject of the drawing seems to be a version of the popular Pre-Raphaelite theme of Paolo and Francesca. The presence of Elizabeth Siddal as the model for the woman dates the drawing 1850–1. After that date she was almost exclusively Rossetti's model.

156 🦎 JEAN FRANÇOIS MILLET 1814–1875

Study of two figures
Red chalk, touched with white, some traces of black chalk. 172 × 236 mm
Stamped with the artist's studio stamp 'J.F.M.'; verso: 2 studies in pencil, perhaps for *Hagar*; sketch of a limb in red chalk
Collection: Ricketts and Shannon (no. 2125)
Reference: *Cent dessins français du Fitzwilliam Museum* (1976) no. 65

The drawing previously belonged to William Perkins Babcock (1826–1899), a painter from Boston who lived at Barbizon in 1853 and was a friend and admirer of Millet.

157 🦎 JEAN FRANÇOIS MILLET 1814–1875

Le Vanneur
Black chalk. 198 × 162 mm
Collection: Ricketts and Shannon (no. 2124); bought by Ricketts from the Leicester Galleries, Leicester Square, London, in 1906

None of the three versions of this subject of winnowing corresponds to this drawing. Ricketts specifically praises Millet's figures seen at work: 'Millet's work is placid and brooding in temper: he expresses all the gravity of work and the gravity of repose.'

158 🐦 JEAN FRANÇOIS MILLET 1814–1875

The Shepherdess
Reed pen and ink on squared buff paper. 196 × 227 mm
Collection: Ricketts and Shannon (no. 2122)

In *The Shepherdess with her Flock*, which Millet showed at the Paris 1867
Exhibition, the shepherdess is standing by her flock, not driving it. This
drawing, although squared up, does not seem to have been used for a
larger work.

159 🐦 GIOVANNI ANTONIO PORDENONE
1483–1539

Man standing holding a staff
Black and red chalk. 214 × 115 mm
Inscribed verso in black ink 'Pordenone', lower left of mount 'Zuccaro'
and 'A member of the Papal Guard'
Collection: Ricketts and Shannon (no. 2133)

The dry style of this drawing suggests an early date, before Pordenone's
visit to Venice.

160 🐦 FRANCESCO PRIMATICCIO 1504–1570

Death of Agamemnon and Cassandra
Red chalk, heightened with white on red tinted paper, traces of
squaring. 225 × 186 mm
Collection: Ricketts and Shannon (no. 2134); Sotheby's, 1 November
1920, lot 83, as *Massacre of the Innocents*

The drawing was listed in the collection as *The Rape of the Sabines*.
The present title is due to Mlle Sylvie Béguin, who points out that it
relates to the left-hand section of Primaticcio's design for *The Murder
of Agamemnon and Cassandra* in the Galérie d'Ulysse at Fontainebleau.
A drawing for the other half of the composition is in the National
Museum, Stockholm.

161 🐦 PUVIS DE CHAVANNES 1824–1898 (see pl. 23)

A study for *Le Travail*
Pencil, black and red chalk, squaring in pencil. 597 × 577 mm

Signed in red chalk lower right 'à Antoine Vallon / P. Puvis de Chavannes'
Collection: Ricketts and Shannon (no. 2135)

A study for two figures seen in the left background of the mural *Le Travail*, exhibited at the Salon in 1863 and now in the Musée de Picardie at Amiens.

Ricketts' view of Puvis was that in his work 'man figures in the eternally engrossing drama of work and repose, effort or thought, under the spell of passion, tenderness and meditation; in movements of efforts and moods of compassion...god-like workmen and mothers of *Le Travail* and *Le Repos*...'

162 ☙ PUVIS DE CHAVANNES 1824–1898

A study for *The Prodigal Son*
Charcoal on tracing paper, squared for transfer. 421 × 322 mm
Collection: Ricketts and Shannon (no. 2137)

The drawing is a study for a painting exhibited at the Salon, 1879. Three related paintings exist.

163 ☙ PUVIS DE CHAVANNES 1824–1898

Satyr holding a staff
Pencil on buff paper, squared for enlargement. 138 × 84 mm
Collection: Ricketts and Shannon (no. 2136)

The drawing may be connected with *Ludus pro Patria* in the Museum at Amiens.

164 ☙ REMBRANDT VAN RIJN 1606–1669 (see pl. 24)

Outskirts of a town with walls and a doorway
Pen and indian ink with brown wash. 152 × 143 mm
Collection: Ricketts and Shannon (no. 2138)
Literature: includes Otto Benesch, *Rembrandt* I, 57a, fig. 519

This is the earliest known landscape drawing by Rembrandt, datable *c.* 1627–8, in the Leiden period. Benesch points out that the small vertical figures recall those in the work of Pynas, Lastman, and Italianate Dutch landscape painters. The attribution stands by itself: there are no comparable drawings.

67

165 🐦 REMBRANDT VAN RIJN 1606–1669 (see pl. 25)

The Supper at Emmaus
Pen and brown ink, brown wash, heightened with white. 198 × 183 mm
Inscribed verso in ink 'Rembrant' [sic] and numbered 2328; old mount inscribed, in a similar hand to the numbering, 'de Emmausgangers'
Collection: Ricketts and Shannon (no. 2139)
Literature: includes Otto Benesch, *Rembrandt*, IV, C47, pl. 1017; J. Rosenberg in *Art Bulletin* LXI (March 1959), p. 116

The present drawing is related to a print inscribed 'Rembrandt f.1635', but it is dramatised by the rays of light over Christ's chair being used as the focus of Christ's miraculous appearance. The composition goes back to the earliest drawing of the subject, dated by Benesch *c.* 1629. The drawing's attribution is accepted by Rosenberg and Lugt, but not unhesitatingly by Benesch. *Pentimenti* in Christ's chair, the seated disciple seen as a solid silhouette, and the effects of light argue for the attribution to Rembrandt himself.

166 🐦 REMBRANDT VAN RIJN 1606–1669 (see pl. 26)

The Agony in the Garden
Pen and brown ink, brown wash. 196 × 190 mm
Inscribed verso in pencil 'Adams no. 11 3–5'
Collection: Ricketts and Shannon (no. 2140)
Reference: *European Drawings from the Fitzwilliam* (1976–7) no. 82, p. 51, pl. 82

The drawing dates either from the 1650s or, possibly, from the 1640s; the outer limits are *c.* 1648 to 1655. An incomplete date on the closely related etching of the same subject argues for a date in the 1650s.

167 🐦 GUIDO RENI 1575–1642

Study for a Virgin and Child
Black chalk with faint traces of white heightening, slightly rubbed. Lower right corner of the sheet cut off. 383 × 255 mm
Collection: Ricketts and Shannon (no. 2046)
Reference: *European Drawings from the Fitzwilliam* (1976–7) no. 67, p. 42, pl. 67 (as van Dyck)

The drawing was attributed formerly to van Dyck. Michael Jaffé had already pointed out its debt to Guido Reni before Catherine Johnston, in a letter to the Museum of 11 April 1977, identified it as a study for Reni's lost Tanari Madonna. Dr Johnston's attribution is supported by the existence of an engraving after the lost painting by Mauro Gandolfi and by a drawing of it made by Lodovico Borini.

168   JOSE RIBERA (CALLED LO
                SPAGNOLETTO) 1591–1652

Head of a Virgin
Red chalk, pasted down. 192 × 168 mm
Inscribed on mount, centre below 'Ribera'
Collection: Ricketts and Shannon (no. 2143)

The pose of the Virgin's head in this drawing may be compared with that in the Pietà painted by Ribera for the Convent of San Martino, Naples, in 1637.

169   AUGUSTE RODIN   1840–1917

Achilles and Cheiron
Pencil, black chalk, brown wash, heightened with white on cream faded paper. 116 × 126 mm
Signed in ink in top left corner 'A Rodin'
Collection: Ricketts and Shannon (no. 2144)

Possibly fragments of a battle between Lapiths and Centaurs, after the antique.

170   AUGUSTE RODIN   1840–1917 (see pl. 27)

The Shades approaching Dante and Virgil
Pencil, pen and dark sepia wash on buff paper. 183 × 117 (irregular) mm
Signed lower centre 'A Rodin'
Collection: Ricketts and Shannon (no. 2145); bought from the Carfax Gallery
Reference: *Cent dessins français du Fitzwilliam Museum* (1976) no. 89

171 🦎 AUGUSTE RODIN 1840–1917

Charity
Pen and body colour on buff paper. 120 × 111 mm
Signed lower right corner 'A Rodin'
Collection: Ricketts and Shannon (no. 2146)

172 🦎 DANTE GABRIEL ROSSETTI 1828–1882

Elizabeth Siddal, seated at a window
Pencil, rubbed perhaps with a stump, with some pen and indian ink.
234 × 180 mm irregular, laid down
Dated bottom left 'hastings June 1854'
Collection: Ricketts and Shannon (no. 2147)
Literature: H. C. Marillier, *Dante Gabriel Rossetti* (1899) p. 258, cat. no.
327: Virginia Surtees, *The Paintings and Drawings of Dante Gabriel
Rossetti* (1971) no. 466, pl. 429

Elizabeth Siddal was the model for most of Rossetti's early watercolours
and for all the Beatrices, except the last. She became his fiancée in 1854
and his wife in 1860, and died in 1862.

Ricketts wrote in a letter (April 1918), 'We have added two charming
Rossetti studies of Miss Siddal to our treasures; they are feeble in
workmanship but quite exquisite in feeling; then, we have all, when
young, been in love with Miss Siddal (Mrs Rossetti).'

173 🦎 DANTE GABRIEL ROSSETTI 1828–1882

Elizabeth Siddal, reading
Pencil, rubbed perhaps with a stump, with some pen and indian ink.
242 × 290 mm
Dated bottom left 'hastings / June 2 1854'
Collection: Ricketts and Shannon (no. 2155)
Exhibitions: include Royal Academy *Dante Gabriel Rossetti* (1973) no.
187
Literature: H. C. Marillier, *op. cit.* p. 258, cat. no. 327; Virginia Surtees,
op. cit. no. 465

174 🦎 DANTE GABRIEL ROSSETTI 1828–1882 (see
pl. 28)

Mary Magdalene at the door of Simon the Pharisee
Pen and indian ink on paper, mounted on fine linen on a stretcher; a

strip of paper about one inch in width has been added to the foot of
the drawing. 508 × 457 mm irregular
Monogram, and date lower right '1858'
Collection: Ricketts and Shannon (no. 2151)
Exhibitions: include Royal Academy *Dante Gabriel Rossetti* (1973) no.
115
Literature: includes H. C. Marillier, *op. cit.* no. 78, pp. 50, 63, 97, 99;
Virginia Surtees, *op. cit.* no. 109

One of Rossetti's most important drawings, for many years lost but
rediscovered and bought by Ricketts before 1890. The subject is used
by Rossetti for a poem. There are thirteen related drawings and two
replicas.

175   DANTE GABRIEL ROSSETTI   1828–1882

Golden Water
Body colour on paper, laid on fine linen on a stretcher. 365 × 187 mm
slightly irregular
Monogram, and date lower right '1858' (?)
Collection: Ricketts and Shannon (no. 2148)
Literature: Virginia Surtees, *op. cit.* repr. pl. 149

The subject is taken from the *Arabian Nights* story of two sisters who
were jealous of their younger sister, Princess Parisade, depicted here
carrying a black barrel containing the golden water.

176   DANTE GABRIEL ROSSETTI   1828–1882

Study for *The Salutation of Beatrice*
Pencil on paper, mounted on card. 251 × 254 mm
Collection: Ricketts and Shannon (no. 2154)
Literature: Virginia Surtees, *op. cit* pl. 178

This drawing is one of the studies for an oil painting for a cabinet at
the Red House, Bexley Heath, the home of William Morris. The
painting is in the National Gallery of Canada. Eight other drawings
related to the design are listed by Surtees.

177 🐟 THOMAS ROWLANDSON   1757–1827 (see pl. 29)

Boats off a jetty
Pen and ink and watercolour on paper laid down on card. 275 × 302 mm, card 330 × 360 mm
Collection: Ricketts and Shannon (no. 2169)

An almost identical scene with slight differences at the left is in Birmingham, signed, and inscribed 'Pier at Amsterdam' and dated 1792.

178 🐟 THOMAS ROWLANDSON   1757–1827

Woodyeats Inn
Pencil, pen and black ink, and watercolour on paper made up of three pieces stuck down on card, and completed by colouring the card upper right. 251 × 425 mm irregular, card 288 × 461 mm
Inscribed in ink lower left 'Woodyeats Inn Between Blandford and Salisbury'
Collection: Ricketts and Shannon (no. 2158)

Six Rowlandson drawings were bought for the collection in 1925.

179 🐟 THOMAS ROWLANDSON   1757–1827

The Paris Diligence (leaving 'Le Cocque en Pate' Inn)
Pen and ink and watercolours. 232 × 364 mm
Signed bottom left 'T Rowlandson'
Collection: Ricketts and Shannon (no. 2165)

This drawing is a variant of an engraving by Rowlandson published by T. Tegg, 1810.

180 🐟 THOMAS ROWLANDSON   1757–1827 (see pl. 30)

A windy day at Temple Bar
Pen and ink and watercolour. 279 × 419 mm
Collection: Ricketts and Shannon (no. 2164)

181 ✍ SIR PETER PAUL RUBENS 1577–1640 (see pl. 31)

Two men wrestling
Charcoal, pen and bistre ink, point of the brush, brown wash, heightened with white and yellow ochre on buff paper. 235 × 366 mm
Inscribed on the backing in ink 'J. C. Robinson 1878' and in pencil 'Potidone (?) 16'
Collection: Ricketts and Shannon (no. 2181); formerly Sir J. C. Robinson
Reference: *European Drawings from the Fitzwilliam* (1976–7) no. 86, p. 54, pl. 86

This drawing, previously called *Hercules and Anteus*, is one of several studies based on the antique marble of *Two Wrestlers* in the Uffizi. The drawing presumably dates from Rubens' stay in Rome, 1605–8. Later restoration of the group makes it difficult to say how close the original is to Rubens' subject. The artist has improvised a dramatic action from a static marble original.

182 ✍ SIR PETER PAUL RUBENS 1577–1640 (see pl. 32)

Two figure studies: recto, two men in cloaks, one with a large-brimmed hat; verso, drapery study for St Francis Xavier
Black chalk on damaged paper. 415 × 241 mm
Inscribed in ink top left corner, in Rubens' hand (?), 'de Backere'; in ink bottom left, in Padre Resta's hand, '[A]nnibale Carracci, ma / Studio di Rubens / Habe scol.° di Vandic[k] / [l'hab or eb]bi in Roma nella morta d'un Fiamen[go]...suo herede'
Collection: Ricketts and Shannon (no. 2176); bought by Ricketts at Christie's, 14 May 1902 (part of 348, £5)
Literature: includes Michael Jaffé, 'The Interest of Rubens in Annibale and Agostino Carracci, Further Notes', in *Burlington Magazine* vol. 99 (November 1957) figs. 18 and 19; J. S. Held, *Rubens: Selected Drawings* (1959) under no. 100; L. Burchard and R. A. Hulst, *Rubens Drawings* (Brussels 1963) no. 115, pl. 115

The drawing, as Ricketts noticed, is connected with the large altarpiece *The Miracle of St Francis Xavier*, painted for the Jesuit church in Antwerp, and now in the Kunsthistorisches Museum, Vienna. This drawing may have been drawn between the preliminary oil sketch and the finished picture, whose date is *c.* 1618.

183 🐚 SIR PETER PAUL RUBENS 1577–1640

Study of a kneeling male figure, seen from behind
Charcoal, heightened with white on buff paper. 375 × 285 mm
Collection: Ricketts and Shannon (no. 2177)
Reference: *European Drawings from the Fitzwilliam* (1976–7) no. 87, p. 55, pl. 87

For Ricketts, Rubens was 'one of the world's two supreme draughtsmen, one of the men who never forgot the continuous quality of form as it exists round and over the human body'.
   A suggested connection of this drawing is with the *Miracle of St Walpurga*, formerly part of the predella of the *Elevation of the Cross* of 1610–11 in Antwerp Cathedral. The drawing may be dated within the first decade of Rubens' return to Antwerp from Italy in 1608.

184 🐚 SIR PETER PAUL RUBENS 1577–1640

A Path Bordered by Trees
Traces of preliminary work in black chalk, tip of the brush and brown ink, strengthened with the pen and black ink, brown wash heightened with white, except for a strip at the right which shows a few outlines only; on white paper which has been covered with brown wash, except on certain highlights at the right; joined vertically in the centre. 313 × 403 mm
Inscribed verso in ink 'T. Kerrich 1767 / M. C. C.' (Magdalene College Cambridge)
Collection: Ricketts and Shannon (no. 2178); formerly the Rev. Thomas Kerrich (1748–1828)
Reference: *European Drawings from the Fitzwilliam* (1976–7) no. 88, p. 35, pl. 88

Some of Barocci's landscape studies were available to Rubens' buying agents before 1616, around which date this drawing may be placed. Michael Jaffé remarks the Baroccesque character of the delicate and atmospheric handling.

185 🐚 SIR PETER PAUL RUBENS 1577–1640 (see pl. 33)

Study for Mary Magdalene
Charcoal on buff paper. 262 × 402 mm
Inscribed, recto in ink on the right '114' and in pencil lower left

74

'P. P. Rubens'; verso in ink on the right 'No 1 Vp65', in ink on the left 'No. 1'
Collection: Ricketts and Shannon (no. 2182)
Reference: *European Drawings from the Fitzwilliam* (1976–7) no. 89, p. 56, pl. 89

This figure is closely related to Mary Magdalene in the *Lamentation over the Dead Christ*, painted for Charles, Duc d'Arenberg, *c.* 1620, as an altarpiece for the church of the Capuchins in Brussels, and now in the Musées-Royaux des Beaux Arts, Brussels (no. 380)

186 JACOPO DEL SELLAIO 1441/2–1493

Virgin Adoring the Child
Tempera on wood. 739 × 495 mm
Collection: Ricketts and Shannon (no. 2186)
Reference: Fitzwilliam Museum, *Catalogue of Paintings* II (1967) pp. 152 and 153

The figure of the Virgin, recalling that of the artist's *Annunciation* in Santa Lucia dei Magnoli, Florence, painted in 1473, suggests a late date for this panel.

187 ALFRED STEVENS 1817–1875

Leonard W. Collmann
Oil on canvas. 460 × 353 mm
Collection: Ricketts and Shannon (no. 2228)
Reference: Fitzwilliam Museum, *Catalogue of Paintings* III (1977) pp. 255 and 256, pl. 44

Leonard Collmann (b. *c.* 1816, d. before 1891) was an architect and decorator and a friend of Stevens.

The painting cost £300, a major purchase for the two artists, but its justification was that according to Ricketts it was 'one of his masterpieces'. In another passage he wrote, 'We were delighted with the Alfred Stevens portrait of Collman; we also understand the rumour that it resembled Shannon's painting; at its birth, Titian and Ingres stood sponsors; at the birth of Shannon, Titian and Velasquez.'

188 ⚡ ALFRED STEVENS 1817–1875

Study for the Wellington monument
Pencil, pen, and watercolours. 320 × 250 mm
Collection: Ricketts and Shannon (no. 2216)

Stevens' first designs for the Wellington monument date from 1856/7.
    A large group of Stevens drawings was acquired for the collection from a sale at which Sir Edmund Davis was a competing bidder. Ricketts classed Stevens with Ingres: 'there have been artists who have ventured to compete with the great Italians in the study of form, whose art moves to a rhythm, such as Ingres and Alfred Stevens...'

189 ⚡ ALFRED STEVENS 1817–1875

Study for an illustrated Bible
Pen and brown ink. 230 × 159 mm
Collection: Ricketts and Shannon (no. 2222 c)

This is a study for St John's Gospel, chapter 21.

190 ⚡ ALFRED STEVENS 1817–1875

Study for a silver jug
Pen and grey wash. 216 × 242 mm
Inscribed verso in pencil 'Alfred Stevens. Study for a silver jug.'
Collection: Ricketts and Shannon (no. 2213(2))

191 ⚡ ALFRED STEVENS 1817–1875

Study for a prophet in St Paul's
Red chalk. 318 × 261 mm
Verso: pencil studies for a Resurrection
Collection: Ricketts and Shannon (no. 2202)

This and other Stevens drawings were probably bought at Hodson's auction rooms, where in 1906 Ricketts recorded having failed to buy Pre-Raphaelite works: 'I had already spent too much on Legros and Stevens drawings.' Stevens worked on St Paul's from 1862 till his death.

192 SIR JAMES THORNHILL 1675–1734

Study for a staircase decoration
Pen and ink and bistre. 388 × 293 mm
Collection: Ricketts and Shannon (no. 2234)

The designs show scenes from the life of Julius Caesar.

193 GIOVANNI BATTISTA TIEPOLO 1696–1770

Study of a female nude, seated on clouds, seen from below, right arm
raised
Pen and dark brown ink, dark brown wash. 279 × 193 mm
Inscribed in ink lower left-hand corner '35'
Collection: Ricketts and Shannon (no. 2238)

It is doubtful whether Ricketts and Shannon would have acquired many
drawings by Tiepolo if they had not been offered an exchange by Sir
Edmund Davis. Ricketts recorded on 5 November 1903, 'Spent most
of the day with Davis hanging pictures. He presented us with a batch
of Tiepolos he did not like, and we swapped two Claude drawings
against the others, some seven Tiepolos in all!'
   This drawing is a study for an angel in *Triumph of Faith*, in the Chiesa
della Pietà, Venice.

194 GIOVANNI BATTISTA TIEPOLO 1696–1770
    (see pl. 34)

Study of a building with a loggia at left, seen over a wall
Pen and dark brown ink, dark brown wash. 125 × 221 mm
Collection: Ricketts and Shannon (no. 2240)
Literature: Rodolfo Palluchini, 'Un gruppo di disegni inediti di
Giambattista Tiepolo', *La Critica d'Arte* no. 7 (February 1937) pp. 41–2,
fig. 1

195 GIOVANNI BATTISTA TIEPOLO 1696–1770
    (see pl. 35)

Study of a farmhouse with a vine to right
Pen and dark brown wash. 110 × 313 mm
Collection: Ricketts and Shannon (no. 2241)
Literature: Rodolfo Palluchini, 'Un gruppo di disegni inediti di
Giambattista Tiepolo', *La Critica d'Arte* no. 7 (February 1937) pp. 41–2,
fig. 2

196 GIOVANNI BATTISTA TIEPOLO 1696–1790

Reclining female figure, seated on clouds, holding a jar
Pen and dark brown ink, grey-brown wash over some pencil. 201 × 155 mm
Collection: Ricketts and Shannon (no. 2245)

A female river deity has been suggested as the subject, and Domenico Tiepolo has been proposed as the draughtsman.

197 GIOVANNI DOMENICO TIEPOLO
1727–1804

A crowd of Orientals
Pen and light brown ink, light brown wash. 216 × 347 mm
Collection: Ricketts and Shannon (no. 2246); from Sir Edmund Davis

The subject matter is reminiscent of Giambattista's etchings *Scherzi di Fantasia*.

198 JACOPO ROBUSTI, IL TINTORETTO
1518–1594 (see pl. 36)

Study of a kneeling male nude figure with arms outstretched
Charcoal on grey paper. 190 × 190 mm
Inscribed in ink lower right-hand corner 'G Tintoretto', in the same hand as no. 2248
Collection: Ricketts and Shannon (no. 2254); formerly Sir Joshua Reynolds
Exhibition: Fitzwilliam Museum *15th- and 16th-Century Drawings* (1960) no. 52
Literature: H. Tietze and E. Tietze-Conrat, *The Drawings of the Venetian Painters* (New York 1944) p. 279, no. 1574

The drawing does not seem to be connected with any known painting.

199 JACOPO ROBUSTI, IL TINTORETTO
1518–1594 (see pl. 37)

Leaning figure of an oarsman with a pole
Brush and brown ink worked over charcoal on blue paper. 185 × 250 mm

Collection: Ricketts and Shannon (no. 2247)
Reference: *European Drawings from the Fitzwilliam* (1976–7) no. 44
Literature: Tietze and Tietze-Conrat, *op. cit.* p. 379, no. 1571, pl. CVIII

A study for the oarsman in the middle distance in the *Battle of Legnano* of *c.* 1579, now in the Alte Pinakothek, Munich.

200  JACOPO ROBUSTI, IL TINTORETTO
1518–1594

Study of a seated male nude
Charcoal on buff paper squared for enlargement and transfer. 302 × 208 mm
Inscribed in ink lower right-hand corner 'G. Tint[oretto]', in the same hand as on many drawings by Tintoretto or his school. Verso: the same figure in the opposite direction, perhaps traced from the recto
Collection: Ricketts and Shannon (no. 2253); formerly Sir Joshua Reynolds
Exhibitions: London, Goldsmiths' Hall *Treasures of Cambridge* (1959) no. 61; Fitzwilliam Museum *15th- and 16th-Century Drawings* (1960) no. 51
Literature: Tietze and Tietze-Conrat, *op. cit.* p. 279, no. 1572

The posture of the figure resembles Christ in *Christ in the House of Mary and Martha* (Munich no. 1130) and Christ in *Christ Crowning the Virgin* in San Giorgio Maggiore, Venice.

Four drawings by Tintoretto were in the collection by 1915.

201  ATTRIBUTED TO JACOPO ROBUSTI, IL
TINTORETTO 1518–1594

Standing figure of a man
Charcoal on buff paper. 374 × 217 mm
Inscribed bottom right 'G Tintoretto', in the same hand as no. 2254
Collection: Ricketts and Shannon (no. 2248)
Literature: Tietze and Tietze-Conrat, *op. cit.* no. 1767 as 'Tintoretto shop'

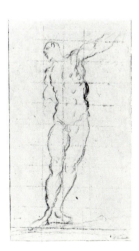

The drawing may be related to *Moses* in the Scuolo di San Rocco, Venice.

A mythological couple in embrace
Charcoal and black chalk, on faded blue paper. 252 × 260 mm
Collection: Ricketts and Shannon (no. 2256); formerly (?) Sir P. P.
Rubens; J. Richardson Sr
Reference: *European Drawings from the Fitzwilliam* (1976–7) no. 45

The attribution to Titian, made by Ricketts, c. 1925, has been accepted
generally. The drawing has been assigned to the years 1550–5. Michael
Jaffé has proposed a considerably later date, c. 1570, by comparison with
the X-ray evidence of the painting of *Tarquin and Lucretia* in the
Fitzwilliam Museum, engraved by C. Cort, 1572, and with the (?)
unfinished painting of the same theme in the Akademie der Bildenden
Künste, Vienna, of c. 1570. A copy of the present drawing, in the Louvre
(inv. no. 5660), was published in error for the original by F. Wickhoff
(*Kunstgeschichtliches Jahrbuch der Zentralcommission* III (1909) p. 24, pl. III).
Inscribed 'Titiaen', that has been convincingly attributed to Jordaens
by Bert W. Meijer (*Hommage à Titien* (Institut Néerlandais, Paris 1976)
pp. 27–8, no. 16). Jordaens was never in Italy; and he derived any
knowledge of Titian drawings from his contact with Rubens. This
circumstance, together with the existence of a free adaptation c. 1617
of Titian's design of the couple in embrace by Rubens in his *Rape of
the Daughters of Leucippus* (Alte Pinakothek, Munich), points to the
strong probability that the Fitzwilliam drawing was once part of
Rubens' collection.

In Ricketts' eyes, Titian was the father of modern painting. A chapter
of his book on the artist was about Titian's rare extant drawings, and
the attribution of this sheet to Titian represents a high point in Ricketts'
connoisseurship. He entitled it *Jupiter and Io*.

203 🦎 ATTRIBUTED TO ANDREA DEL VERROCCHIO 1435–1488 (see pl. 39)

The Infant Christ
Black chalk, heightened with white on buff paper (worn in many
places). 268 × 235 mm
Collection: Ricketts and Shannon (no. 2260); bought in 1904

At first Ricketts thought this fragment was by Lorenzo di Credi, but
in 1914 he changed his mind, to describe it as 'under the faint influence
of Verrocchio and Leonardo'. Then, as he wrote on 20 February 1914,
'Siren brought photographs of Leonardo drawings. There is no doubt
that our drawing of a child, which hitherto I have considered a work

by Credi under the influence of Leonardo is a study or part of a cartoon made in preparation for the Benois Leonardo in St Petersburgh. So Shannon is right and I was wrong.'

204 🦎 ANTOINE WATTEAU 1684–1721 (see pl. 40)

A man playing a flute
Aux trois crayons on buff paper, pasted down. Repairs to upper right-hand and lower right corner. 170 × 173 mm
Collection: Ricketts and Shannon (no. 2265)
Reference: *European Drawings from the Fitzwilliam* (1976–7) no. 119, p. 75, pl. 11

Since its discovery by Ricketts and Shannon in 1903, the authorship of the drawing has not been in doubt. The figure is one used by the artist in more than one of his paintings and may be compared with the left-hand figure on a sheet of studies in the British Museum (inv. no. 1868.8.8.1274) which represents a flautist full length, in the same pose, but with the head only lightly indicated.

Ricketts wrote of Watteau, 'his gift, his secret is a sense of grace. A vague and languid harmony murmurs in an undertone beneath the wit and fancy of his painting: we feel that his actors must vanish with the sunset, and the lute, which Viola or Silvia touched but now, forget its music.' He was jubilant over acquiring this particular drawing and wrote to Michael Field in 1903, 'God has prepared one charming thing for us in the shape of an important Watteau drawing we bought yesterday. It represents a flute player with intelligent hands, I think a portrait...'

205 🦎 ANTOINE WATTEAU 1684–1721

Antoine de la Roque
Red chalk on paper. 244 × 165 mm
Collection: Ricketts and Shannon (no. 2266)
Reference: *European Drawings from the Fitzwilliam* (1976–7) no. 122, p. 76, pl. 122

Antoine de la Roque (1672–1744) published the first obituary of his friend Watteau in *Le Mercure* after his death in July 1721. The identification of this drawing is based on comparison with an engraved portrait by Bernard Lepicié (1685–1755). De la Roque lost a leg at Malplaquet in 1709.

81

206 ANTOINE WATTEAU 1684–1721

Isabella Brant (after Rubens)
Red, black and white chalk. 188 × 128 mm
Collection: Ricketts and Shannon (no. 2267)
Reference: *European Drawings from the Fitzwilliam* (1976–7) no. 118, p. 74

Ricketts and Shannon owned two drawings after old masters by Watteau. This was first published by Colvin as a copy after Rubens, although he was mistaken about its derivation, which is from a portrait of Isabella Brant in the Uffizi (or some repetition of it). The drawing is in three chalks (*aux trois crayons*), a technique also used by Rubens.

207 ANTOINE WATTEAU 1684–1721 (see pl. 41)

Adam de Coster (after van Dyck)
Red and black chalk, with bistre and sanguine wash. 150 × 100 mm
Collection: Ricketts and Shannon (no. 2271); given to Ricketts by Robert Ross in February 1905
Reference: *Cent dessins français du Fitzwilliam Museum* (1976) no. 94

This is a copy after van Dyck's drawing in the Städelsche Institut, Frankfurt (inv. no. 789), engraved by Pieter de Jode II (1601–1674). It may have been drawn when the original was in the collection of Pierre Crozat (1661–1740), many of whose drawings Watteau copied; but it also shows evidence of Watteau's knowledge of the engraving, which, like Watteau's copy, is more worked up in the lower part than the original drawing.

208 ANTOINE WATTEAU 1684–1721

Lady standing, her back turned towards the spectator
Red chalk. 154 × 52 mm
Collection: Ricketts and Shannon (no. 2269); in the collection by 1909
Literature: K. T. Parker and J. Mathey, *Antoine Watteau: Catalogue complet de son oeuvre dessiné* (Paris 1958) vol. II, no. 558, p. 310 (repr.)

The drawing was engraved by Esmé Jeaurat (1688–1738) *c.* 1735.

209   SIR DAVID WILKIE   1785–1841

Study of a seated woman
Pencil and watercolour. 223 × 184 mm
Collection: Ricketts and Shannon (no. 2274)

This is a sketch for the portrait of Lady Lyndhurst in Spanish dress, completed in 1830.

210   SIR DAVID WILKIE   1785–1841

Tavern scene
Pen and ink and watercolour. 209 × 244 mm
Collection: Ricketts and Shannon (no. 2279 A)

This is similar in style to a series of pen and watercolour studies of 1835.

211   SIR DAVID WILKIE   1785–1841

The Proclamation
Pen and ink and watercolour. 252 × 166 mm
Inscribed verso 'David Wilkie R.A'
Collection: Ricketts and Shannon (no. 2279 B)

Traditionally called *The Proclamation*, this may well be a drawing of *Columbus discovering land*.

ORIENTAL ART

212   INDIAN, 17TH CENTURY

Portrait head
Gouache. 311 × 249 mm
Collection: British Museum (inv. no. 1937.7.10.0334)

213   SUZUKI HARUNOBU   d. 1770

The bush clover from *Beauties of the floating world, young girls and flowers*
Woodcut. 280 × 215 mm
Collection: British Museum (inv. no. 1937.7.10.027)

214   SUZUKI HARUNOBU   d. 1770

Woman with boy carrying fishing net
Woodcut. 273 × 203 mm
Collection: British Museum (inv. no. 1937.7.10.03)

215   SUZUKI HARUNOBU   d. 1770

Two lovers at Yatsuhashi
Woodcut. 269 × 197 mm
Collection: British Museum (inv. no. 1937.7.10.032)

216   KITAGAWA UTAMARO   1753–1806

Man and woman from *Six poets in five colours*
Woodcut. 338 × 229 mm
Collection: British Museum (inv. no. 1937.7.10.089)

217   KITAGAWA UTAMARO   1753–1806

Three beauties standing on a bridge
Woodcut. 365 × 240 mm
Collection: British Museum (inv. no. 1937.7.10.098)

218   KITAGAWA UTAMARO   1753–1806

Yamauba and Kintoki
Woodcut. 368 × 255 mm
Collection: British Museum (inv. no. 1937.7.10.082)

219   KITAGAWA UTAMARO   1753–1806

A woman doing another's hair from *Twelve forms of women's handwork*
Woodcut. 381 × 254 mm
Collection: British Museum (inv. no. 1937.7.10.096)

220   KITAGAWA UTAMARO   1753–1806

Two women and a rope from *A glimpse of beauties round the clock*
Woodcut. 381 × 255 mm
Collection: British Museum (inv. no. 1937.7.10.068)

221 🐉 HOSODA EISHI 1756–1829

Two beauties on a boat (first part of a triptych)
Woodcut. 375 × 249 mm
Collection: British Museum (inv. no. 1937.7.10.059)

222 🐉 ATTRIBUTED TO KIUZAN GAKUTEI
(worked first half of 19th century)

Two ladies holding a koto and a shakuhashi
Woodcut. 146 × 187 mm
Collection: British Museum (inv. no. 1937.7.10.0244)

223 🐉 SCHOOL OF HOKUSAI

Miscellaneous figures. Sketch
Ink on paper. 263 × 285 mm
Collection: British Museum (inv. no. 1937.7.10.0291)

224 🐉 SCHOOL OF HOKUSAI

Tiger
Black ink with red ink squared over. 208 × 205 mm
Collection: Fitzwilliam Museum (no. 3698)

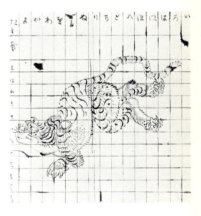

Ricketts and Shannon thought that this drawing and the next two were
by Hokusai.

225 🐉 SCHOOL OF HOKUSAI (see pl. 42)

Tiger
Black ink, wash, and watercolour. 324 × 515 mm
Collection: Fitzwilliam Museum (no. 3956)

226 🐉 SCHOOL OF UTAGAWA (?) (see pl. 43)

The goddess Kwannon
Black ink. 207 × 190 mm
Collection: Fitzwilliam Museum (no. 3968)

227 🐉 KATSUSHIKA HOKUSAI 1760–1849

Samurai and horse
Woodcut. 193 × 262 mm
Collection: British Museum (inv. no. 1937.7.10.0215)

228 🐉 KATSUSHIKA HOKUSAI 1760–1849

Iris
Woodcut. 248 × 349 mm
Collection: British Museum (inv. no. 1937.7.10.0177)

229 🐉 KATSUSHIKA HOKUSAI 1760–1849

Mishima Pass in Kai Province from *Thirty-six views of Mount Fuji*
Woodcut. 254 × 315 mm
Collection: British Museum (inv. no. 1937.7.10.0161)

230 🐉 KATSUSHIKA HOKUSAI 1760–1849

Rainstorm below the mountain from *Thirty-six views of Mount Fuji*
Woodcut. 254 × 378 mm
Collection: British Museum (inv. no. 1937.7.10.0120)

231 🐉 ISODA KORYŪSAI (active later 1760s to early 1780s)

Woman and elephant screen from *Twenty-four examples of filial piety of Yamoto*
Woodcut. 260 × 197 mm
Collection: British Museum (inv. no. 1937.7.10.049)

232 🐉 UTAGAWA HIROSHIGE 1797–1858

Shōno from *Fifty-three stations on the Tōkaidō*
Woodcut. 229 × 349 mm
Collection: British Museum (inv. no. 1937.7.10.0257)

Plate 4: Cat. no. 11

Plate 5: Cat. no. 24

Plate 6: Cat. nos. 45 & 46

Plate 7: Cat. no. 49

Plate 8: Cat. no. 70

Plate 9: Cat. no. 89

Plate 10: Cat. no. 90

Plate 11 : Cat. no. 102

Plate 12: Cat. no. 112

Plate 13 : Cat. no. 116

Plate 14: Cat. no. 122

Plate 15: Cat. no. 125

Plate 16: Cat. no. 128

Plate 17: Cat. no. 129

Plate 19: Cat. no. 132

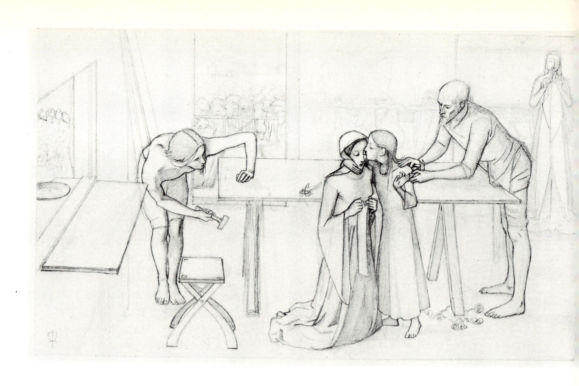

Plate 21: Cat. no. 154

Plate 22: Cat. no. 155

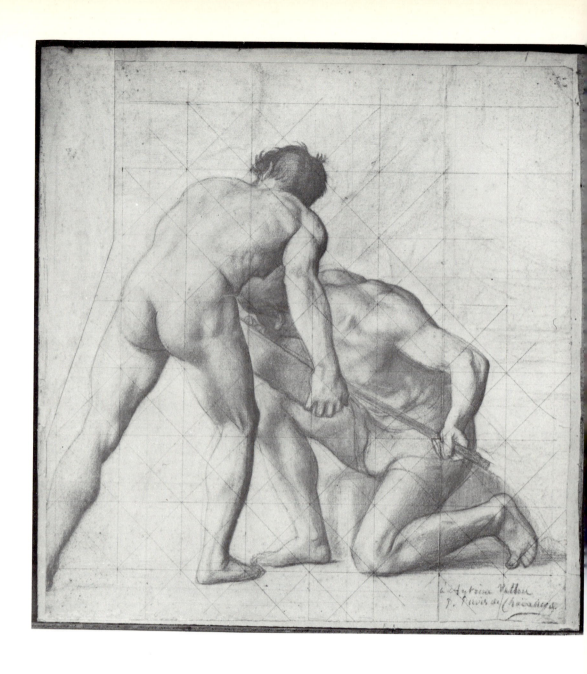

Plate 23: Cat. no. 161

Plate 24: Cat. no. 164

Plate 25: Cat. no. 165

Plate 26: Cat. no. 166

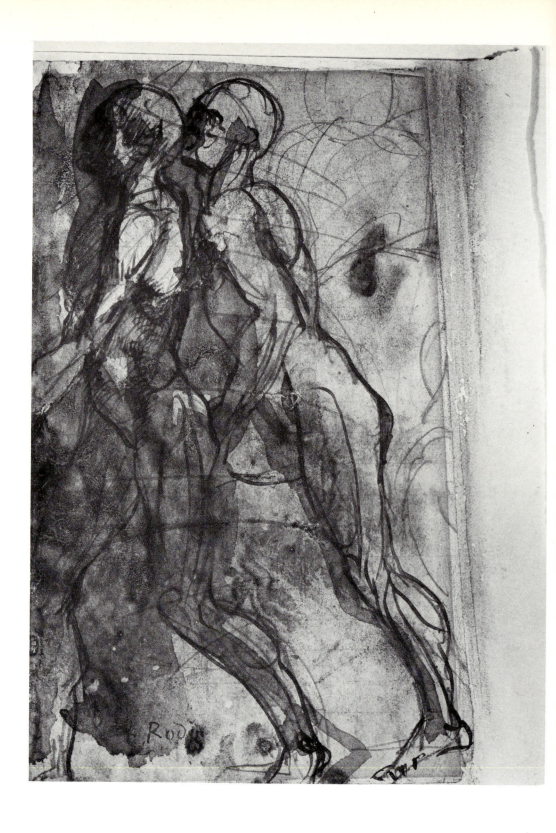

Plate 27: Cat. no. 170

Plate 28: Cat. no. 174

Plate 29: Cat. no. 177

Plate 30: Cat. no. 180

Plate 31: Cat. no. 181

Plate 32: Cat. no. 182

Plate 33: Cat. no. 185

Plate 34: Cat. no. 194

Plate 35: Cat. no. 195

Plate 36: Cat. no. 198

Plate 37: Cat. no. 199

Plate 38: Cat. no. 202

Plate 39: Cat. no. 203

Plate 40: Cat. no. 204

Plate 41: Cat. no. 207

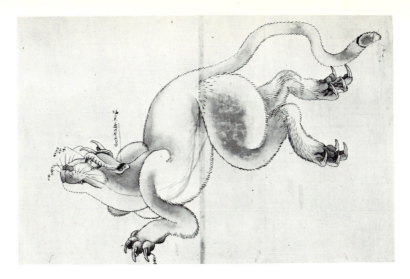

Plate 42: Cat. no. 225

Plate 43: Cat. no. 226